America's Entry into World War I

Donald Murphy, *Book Editor*

Bonnie Szumski, *Publisher*
Scott Barbour, *Managing Editor*

**OPPOSING
VIEWPOINTS®
SERIES**   **AT ISSUE IN HISTORY**

**GREENHAVEN
PRESS®**

THOMSON
——————
GALE

San Diego • Detroit • New York • San Francisco • Cleveland
New Haven, Conn. • Waterville, Maine • London • Munich

THOMSON

GALE

LIBRARY OF CONGRESS CATALOGING-IN-PUBLICATION DATA
America's entry into World War I / Donald Murphy, book editor.
p. cm. — (At issue in history)
Includes bibliographical references and index.
ISBN 0-7377-1792-0 (pbk. : alk. paper) — ISBN 0-7377-1791-2 (alk. paper)
1. World War I, 1914–1918—United States. I. Murphy, Donald, 1936– .
II. Series.
D619.A6497 2004
940.3'73—dc22   2003049495

Printed in the United States of America

Contents

participation. It also needs to institute universal military service.

Chapter 3: The Decision for War

including financiers and arms makers, at the expense of the common people.

Chapter 4: The U.S. Decision to Enter World War I in Retrospect

Foreword

Historian Robert Weiss defines history simply as "a record and interpretation of past events." Both elements—record and interpretation—are necessary, Weiss argues.

> Names, dates, places, and events are the essence of history. But historical writing is not a compendium of facts. It consists of facts placed in a sequence to tell a connected story. A work of history is not merely a story, however. It also must analyze what happened and *why*—that is, it must interpret the past for the reader.

For example, the events of December 7, 1941, that led President Franklin D. Roosevelt to call it "a date which will live in infamy" are fairly well known and straightforward. A force of Japanese planes and submarines launched a torpedo and bombing attack on American military targets in Pearl Harbor, Hawaii. The surprise assault sank five battleships, disabled or sank fourteen additional ships, and left almost twenty-four hundred American soldiers and sailors dead. On the following day, the United States formally entered World War II when Congress declared war on Japan.

These facts and consequences were almost immediately communicated to the American people who heard reports about Pearl Harbor and President Roosevelt's response on the radio. All realized that this was an important and pivotal event in American and world history. Yet the news from Pearl Harbor raised many unanswered questions. Why did Japan decide to launch such an offensive? Why were the attackers so successful in catching America by surprise? What did the attack reveal about the two nations, their people, and their leadership? What were its causes, and what were its effects? Political leaders, academic historians, and students look to learn the basic facts of historical events and to read the intepretations of these events by many different sources, both primary and secondary, in order to develop a more complete picture of the event in a historical context.

In the case of Pearl Harbor, several important questions surrounding the event remain in dispute, most notably the role of President Roosevelt. Some historians have blamed his policies for deliberately provoking Japan to attack in order to propel America into World War II; a few have gone so far as to accuse him of knowing of the impending attack but not informing others. Other historians, examining the same event, have exonerated the president of such charges, arguing that the historical evidence does not support such a theory.

The Greenhaven At Issue in History series recognizes that many important historical events have been interpreted differently and in some cases remain shrouded in controversy. Each volume features a collection of articles that focus on a topic that has sparked controversy among eyewitnesses, contemporary observers, and historians. An introductory essay sets the stage for each topic by presenting background and context. Several chapters then examine different facets of the subject at hand with readings chosen for their diversity of opinion. Each selection is preceded by a summary of the author's main points and conclusions. A bibliography is included for those students interested in pursuing further research. An annotated table of contents and thorough index help readers to quickly locate material of interest. Taken together, the contents of each of the volumes in the Greenhaven At Issue in History series will help students become more discriminating and thoughtful readers of history.

Introduction

On April 2, 1917, President Woodrow Wilson delivered one of the most important speeches in U.S. history. Addressing a special session of Congress, Wilson solemnly stated that the recent actions of the imperial German government were "nothing less than war against the government and people of the United States" and called for Congress to declare war against Germany. Four days later, Congress voted overwhelmingly in favor of entering what became the first world war, ending the United States' long period of neutrality. Since the outbreak of the European conflict in 1914, Wilson had resolutely avoided participating in the war, contending that its "causes and objects" had nothing to do with the United States. He had viewed the war between the Allies (Britain, France, and Russia) and the Central Powers (Germany, Austria-Hungary, and Turkey) as a "blood frenzy of European nationalism"[1] in which neither side held the moral high ground. However, as the fighting continued and Germany took progressively hostile actions against the United States, Wilson ultimately led the country into the war on the side of the Allies. The declaration of war marked the end of the United States' historic policy of isolation from European affairs and the beginning of its transformation into a world political power.

American Isolationism

Since the nineteenth century, the United States had followed a policy of isolation in its relations with Europe. This policy was rooted in the Monroe Doctrine's declaration that the United States would not interfere in European wars and that Europe would stay out of American affairs. In addition, geography contributed to the United States' ability to stay distant from European politics. The Atlantic Ocean insulated the United States from Europe's national battles. Because of this natural buffer, the United States had enjoyed military security at a negligible cost.

Spared even moderate military expenditures for so long, many Americans were hostile to the development of an expensive and strong military. As historian C. Vann Woodward argues, nineteenth-century Americans "came to regard free security much as they did free land and equality, as a natural right."[2] Even on the verge of entering the war in 1917, the U.S. Army was still voluntary and weak, numbering only 5,791 officers and 121,797 enlisted men.

Despite the weakness of its military, the United States was in some ways a great power at the start of World War I. The nation had been transformed by extraordinary industrial growth since the Civil War. In 1914 there were 5 million automobiles and trucks in America. Electric motors were replacing steam engines, and gasoline-driven generators brought energy to remote areas where farmers could now use electric milking machines and light their barns and homes. Cities were growing at an amazing rate. The economy of the United States was almost twice as large as that of its nearest competitor, Germany, and it was growing at a rate that assured its global dominance for many years to come. In addition, it had a population of over 90 million people. However, as historian Robert Tucker points out,

> The resources of a state did not of themselves determine a nation's status. In the then European-dominated state system, the critical test of power was the efficiency and determination with which a state's resources could be mobilized for war. . . . In 1914, the United States had yet to be seriously tested.[3]

The Beginning of War

When war broke out in Europe in the summer of 1914, President Wilson formally proclaimed U.S. neutrality and asked the American people to be "impartial in thought as well as in action." However, from the outset of the war, Wilson's policies favored the Allies. It was this failed policy of "neutrality" that would ultimately lead the United States into war with Germany.

In the earliest days of the war, the United States showed its support for the Allies by exporting a massive quantity of arms and raw material. In 1914 Great Britain had a small army and only a limited capacity to produce weapons. As historians Meirion and Susie Harries argue, without the United States, the British could never have achieved sufficient military strength in a short period of time. Although the United States was officially neutral, it shipped a steady supply of vital resources across the Atlantic. Between August 1914 and August 1917, U.S. Steel supplied more than 6 million tons of steel for military purposes to the Allies. During the same period, the Du Pont corporation increased its supply of explosives to the Allies from half a million to 30 million pounds a month. In 1916 alone, the United States exported $1,290 million in munitions to the Allies.

The Allies also required an enormous amount of food to sustain their field armies and the home population. U.S. beef exports to the Allies rose from 180 million pounds in 1914 to 420 million in 1916. Grain sales more than doubled during the same period. Other crucial exports the United States supplied to the Allies included trucks, cotton, canvas, copper, rubber, submarines, wool, howitzers, rifles, boots, horses, and mules. In contrast to the soaring Anglo-American trade, U.S. exports to the Central Powers plummeted. Whereas U.S. exports to the Allies rose

from $73 million in 1914 to almost $3 billion in 1916, U.S. trade with the Central Powers fell during the same period from $345 million to $29 million.

In addition to supplying more exports to the Allies than to the Central Powers during the period of "neutrality," the Wilson administration also favored the Allies with much greater loans. The United States loaned the Allies $2.3 billion before it made a formal declaration of war while U.S. loans to the Central Powers amounted to only $27 million. In September 1915, Wilson had reversed a previous policy banning America's big banks from extending loans to Allied purchasers of exports. Wilson now allowed bankers to publicly issue loans to finance the booming American trade with the Allies.

British Blockades

One of the reasons that U.S. loans and exports to the Central Powers fell so drastically was the British blockade of German ports in March 1915. With its superior navy, Great Britain was able to cut off sea access to Germany with the goal of preventing supplies from reaching the army and citizens of that country. In this way the Allies aimed to starve the German population into surrendering. Although the blockade violated the rights of the United States, as a neutral country, to trade freely with all participants in the war, President Wilson never made any serious threats of reprisal.

In retaliation against the blockade, and in an increasingly desperate attempt to stop the flow of supplies and weapons from the United States to the Allied countries, Germany began to launch surprise submarine attacks on both merchant and passenger ships that were purported to be carrying war munitions. On May 15, 1915, a German submarine attacked and sank the British passenger liner *Lusitania*, this caused the loss of 124 American lives, severely testing American-German relations. Less than a week later, the Wilson administration issued its first diplomatic response to the sinking, upholding the "indisputable" right of American citizens of a neutral country to travel the high areas and demanding reparations from Germany. Wilson's defense of the United States' rights as a neutral in this case stands in sharp contrast to his failure to enforce these same rights in the country's relations with the Allies. Clearly, the

United States was not pursuing a policy of neutrality but rather favoring the Allies. Nonetheless, Germany, unwilling to provoke the United States, issued an order to submarine commanders to spare passenger liners from torpedo attacks.

Submarine Warfare

Germany restricted its submarine missions for a while, but by the beginning of 1917 the continuing British blockade had contributed to an increasingly desperate situation in the county. During a bitterly cold winter, food was scarce and a cut in the bread rations let to riots in the streets of German cities. Wanting to break the stalemate at sea, German military leaders finally convinced German chancellor Theobald von Bethmann Hollweg to allow a resumption of unrestricted submarine warfare in the Atlantic. According to historian David Kennedy, the German ambassador informed Washington on January 31 that "commencing the next day German submarines would sink on sight and without warning all merchant ships, including neutral vessels, bound for Britain or France."[4]

Despite the Germans' aggressive announcement and the outrage it provoked among U.S. citizens, President Wilson was still extremely reluctant to lead the country into war. However, the United States did break off diplomatic relations with Germany on February 3, 1917. In the next few weeks, German submarines sank four American ships with the loss of fifteen American lives. Because of Germany's challenge to America's rights as a neutral, Wilson found himself forced to enter a war whose consequences he had so long dreaded. Tucker argues that without that challenge, the United States would not have participated in the war:

> Only America's neutral rights could not be sacrificed to peace. Only the right was more precious than peace, its defense being considered inseparable from honor and, in turn, prestige. Without prestige, America would have no standing among the nations. Submission to the German challenge would lead the Allies to dismiss it from those states whose voice and interests must be given serious consideration. The Germans, having faced Wilson down, would look upon the president and the nation he represented with still greater contempt than they had shown in the past.[5]

Wilson was heavily criticized for failing to declare war immediately after Germany's resumption of all-out submarine warfare. British prime minister David Lloyd George exploded when he heard about Wilson' minimal initial response to the German aggression, declaring, "And so he's not going to fight after all! He is awaiting another insult before he actually draws the sword."[6] In Washington, Senator Henry Cabot Lodge stated that Wilson "is afraid" and "flinches in the presence of danger, physical and moral."[7] However, Kennedy argues that Wilson avoided involving the United States in the European war for so long for good reason. In 1917 the United States had just emerged from two decades of political and social upheaval. Progressive reformers had been battling to break the hold of trusts and monopolies that had taken control of the country during the period of industrialization. Indeed, as a progressive reformer, President Wilson had been a major critic of the "money monopoly" and had fought to bring some of the corporations under public control. In addition, the country faced the social problems of increasing labor unrest, government corruption, alcohol abuse, and discrimination against African Americans and women. On top of that, more than 12 million immigrants had arrived in the United States since the turn of the century. Although the country was experiencing a period of huge industrial growth and was prospering in many ways, many aspects of society were unstable. Kennedy writes, "Wilson understandably hesitated to submit the country to the added strain of war."[8] Since the beginning of the war, Americans had disagreed sharply about it and the role the United States should play in it. As Wilson wrote to a friend, "It was necessary for me by very slow stages indeed and with the most genuine purpose to avoid war to lead the country on to single way of thinking."[9] Although many American were still vehemently antiwar, the German attacks finally led Wilson to abandon the traditional policy of American isolationism and at last enter the war. Frank Cobb, and influential newspaper publisher and friend of President Wilson, summed up the United States' new position: "The old isolationism is finished. We are no longer aloof from Europe."[10]

Although the United States officially participated in the war for only nineteen months, the country's entry into the war arguably saved the Allies from defeat. By March 1917, after 337,231 French soldiers had died in the Battle of Verdun and more slaughter had begun near the French city of Reims, French troops were beginning to mutiny. After years of mortgaging itself to American creditors to buy war munitions, Great Britain was only weeks away from a total bankruptcy that might have forced it to agree to peace on the enemy's terms. Because the United States entered the war so late, it was able to provide the money, materials, and manpower necessary to sustain the long-beleaguered Allies until they achieved victory.

Notes

1. Meirion Harries and Susie Harries, *The Last Days of Innocence: America at War, 1917–1918*. New York: Random House, 1997, p. 30.
2. C. Vann Woodward, "The Comparability of American History," in C. Vann Woodward, ed., *The Comparative Approach to American History*. New York: BasicBooks, 1968, pp. 4–5.
3. Robert W. Tucker, "An Inner Circle of One: Woodrow Wilson and His Advisers," *National Interest*, Spring 1998, p. 1.
4. David M. Kennedy, *Over Here: The First World War and American Society*. Oxford, UK: Oxford University Press, 1980, p. 5.
5. Robert W. Tucker, "A Benediction on the Past: Woodrow Wilson's War Address," *World Policy Journal*, Summer 2000.
6. Quoted in Sterling J. Kernek, "Distractions of Peace During War: The Lloyd George Government's Reactions to Woodrow Wilson, December, 1916–November, 1918," *Transactions of the American Philosophical Society*, n.s. 65, part 2 (April 1975), p. 36.
7. Quoted in Arthur S. Link, *Wilson: Campaigns for Progressivism and Peace*. Princeton, NJ: Princeton University Press, 1965, p. 303.
8. Kennedy, *Over Here*, p. 11.
9. Woodrow Wilson to Cleveland H. Dodge, April 4, 1917, Woodrow Wilson Papers, Library of Congress, Washington, DC.
10. Quoted in Robert H. Zieger, *America's Great War: World War I and the American Experience*. Lanham, MD: Rowman & Littlefield, 2000, pp. 55–56.

Chapter **1**

The Issue of American Neutrality

1

American Policy
Favored the Allies

Richard Hofstadter

When war erupted in Europe in 1914, U.S. president Woodrow Wilson determined that the United States should stay out of the conflict. Nearly a pacifist at times, Wilson believed that America should serve as an impartial mediator to help end the war as soon as possible. However, as historian Richard Hofstadter argues in the following selection, Wilson was unable to maintain a neutral stance even in the earliest stages of the war. Hofstadter recounts how the United States sided with the Allies culturally, economically, and diplomatically. Ultimately, Wilson's pro-Allied policies led the United States into a war against Germany. Richard Hofstadter (1916–1970) wrote a number of landmark books about American history, two of which received the Pulitzer Prize: *The Age of Reform* (1955) and *Anti-Intellectualism in American Life* (1963).

[W]oodrow] Wilson grew up when the South was slowly recovering from the ravages of the Civil War; there he had imbibed a horror of violence, which was confirmed by his training in the pacific liberalism of nineteenth-century British thinkers. Professor Charles Callan Tansill in his extremely critical study of Wilson's wartime diplomacy observes that "In the long list of American Chief Executives there is no one who was a more sincere pacifist than the one who led us into war in April, 1917." Yet, as the nation's chief executive, Wilson felt the pull of every

Richard Hofstadter, *The American Political Tradition and the Men Who Made It.* New York: Knopf, 1968. Copyright © 1968 by Alfred A. Knopf, Inc. All rights reserved. Reproduced by permission.

major force that drew the United States toward the conflict.

When Wilson told the people that America must be the example of peace "because peace is the healing and elevating influence of the world and strife is not," he was expressing a deeply ingrained moral bias. "The more I read about the conflict across the seas," he wrote to [businessman] Charles R. Crane in the opening weeks of war, "the more open it seems to me to utter condemnation." Speaking before Congress, he called it "a war with which we have nothing to do." He told [his brother-in-law] Stockton Axson that it would not lead to the permanent settlement of a single problem, and to Colonel [Edward M.] House [Wilson's powerful, unofficial adviser] he predicted that it would "throw the world back three or four centuries." His conception of the proper role of America, as outlined in his speeches, was high-minded. The United States was the only great Western power not involved; it was her duty, her mission, to do something that no other nation had ever done in such a crisis—maintain "absolute self-mastery." Standing aloof from the issues of the conflict, without a single selfish interest, she should make herself ready to serve, to be an impartial mediator, to help bring the war to as early an end as possible, to assist in healing the world's wounds and in preparing for a lasting peace. "It would be a calamity to the world at large," he wrote in an early wartime letter, "if we should be drawn actively into the conflict, and so deprived of all disinterested influence over the settlement."

Wilson's Pro-British Tilt

At the outset Wilson urged that the people be "impartial in thought as well as in action," but he and his most important advisers were utterly incapable of obeying the injunction themselves. One of the signal facts in the train of events leading to American participation was the overwhelming sympathy with the Allies that prevailed in administration circles, and the disposition of Wilson and his counselors to work for an outcome in Europe that would favor the Entente. Wilson's Allied sympathies were as vital as his love of peace. He was a thorough Anglophile. He had learned his greatest lessons from English thinkers; he had taken English statesmen as his models of aspiration and the British Constitution as his model of government; his work as President of Princeton [University] had been, in large measure, an effort to introduce the English idea of a university; even his favorite recreation was to bicycle about the villages of the [English] Lake Country with the *Oxford Book of English Verse* in his pocket. He was surrounded by pro-Ally advisers, especially Robert Lansing, Counselor of the State Department and later Secretary of State, and Colonel House (whom he called "my second personality . . . my independent self"). His Ambassador to England, Walter Hines Page, took it upon himself to represent Britain's cause to America.

One of the signal facts in the train of events leading to American participation was the overwhelming sympathy with the Allies that prevailed in administration circles.

These men were concerned with the prospect of a German victory, which, they felt, would force the United States off the course of its peaceful, progressive development. House wrote to Wilson, August 22, 1914:

> Germany's success will ultimately mean trouble for us. We will have to abandon the path which you are blazing as a standard for future generations, with permanent peace as its goal and a new international ethical code as its guiding star, and build up a military machine of vast proportions.

A week later House recorded in his diary that Wilson had concurred with this analysis, and had gone "even further than I" in his condemnation of Germany's part in the war, including the German people themselves in his indictment. German philosophy, Wilson told him, "was essentially selfish and lacking in spirituality." "England is fighting our fight," Wilson stated in the presence of [Press Secretary Joseph] Tumulty. ". . . I will not take any action to embarrass England when she is fighting for her life and the life of the world." His Attorney General recalled that when some Cabinet members urged him to embargo exports to England early in 1915, he replied:

> Gentlemen, the Allies are standing with their backs to the wall fighting wild beasts. I will permit nothing to be done by our country to hinder or embarrass them

in the prosecution of the war unless admitted rights are grossly violated.

When [U.S. minister to Belgium] Brand Whitlock, visiting him in December 1915, declared: "I am heart and soul for the Allies," Wilson replied: "So am I. No decent man, knowing the situation and Germany could be anything else." If the Germans succeeded, the President predicted to [British ambassador to the United States] Sir Cecil Spring Rice, "we shall be forced to take such measures of defence here as would be fatal to our form of Government and American ideals." In September 1915 he admitted to House that "he had never been sure that we ought not to take part in the conflict and, if it seemed evident that Germany and her militaristic ideas were to win, the obligation upon us was greater than ever."

Neutrality Was Impossible

This feeling, this desire to throw the United States in the scales if necessary to tip the balance of power against Germany, made real neutrality impossible; it caused Wilson to make legalistic discriminations on behalf of the Allies and intensify American economic involvement with them; and in the end he became a prisoner of his own policies. England as well as Germany violated American interests on the high seas and overrode those concepts of international law which the Wilson administration chose to invoke. Both nations were confronted with American protests from time to time, but the protests to Britain were inconclusive, while those to Germany were backed with serious threats. England adopted an extraordinarily sweeping definition of contraband [material subject to seizure by belligerents in war], took astounding liberties with the traditional right of visit and search on the seas at much cost to American shippers, violated traditional concepts of a "legal" blockade, mined the North Sea in a manner intensely obstructive and costly to neutrals, stole American trade with other neutral nations, confiscated valuable American commercial information, and blacklisted American firms that she accused of trading with Germany. But the British diplomats knew that they had administration sympathies (had not Wilson himself told Spring Rice that "a dispute between our two nations would be the crowning calamity"?); Page was present in London to soften the impact of every American protest; and serious action by the United States to enforce its rights against British practices seemed unlikely. As House wrote to Page in October 1914, "I cannot see how there can be any serious trouble between England and America, with all of us feeling as we do."

Growing American Economic Entanglement with the Allies

A critical factor in turning sympathy into open alliance was the growing American economic commitment to the Allies. During 1914 a serious recession had begun in the United States, which showed signs of developing into the first major depression since 1893. However, by 1915 the stimulus of Allied war orders began to be strongly felt; by April 1917 over two billion dollars' worth of goods had been sold to the Allies. America became bound with the Allies in a fateful union of war and prosperity. The Allies' dependence on American supplies gave Wilson an enormous bargaining leverage, which he could have employed to moderate their blockade, but just as [British foreign secretary] Sir Edward Gray chose not to quarrel with his munitions depot, Wilson chose not to quarrel with his country's best customer.

> *"Any little German lieutenant can put us into the war at any time by some calculated outrage."*

In fact, Wilson was made acutely aware of American dependence on Allied war orders. Original Allied purchases drew upon Allied credit balances in the United States, but these were soon exhausted. When the problem arose whether to permit American bankers to make loans to the Allied governments, the administration, acting on [Secretary of State William Jennings] Bryan's thesis that "money is the worst of all contrabands because it commands everything else," refused to encourage the bankers to proceed, and the bankers decided not to act without governmental sanction. However, the urgent Allied need of loans to support continued purchases caused representatives of the National City Bank to reopen the question with Lansing. Both Lansing and Secretary of the Treasury [William G.] McAdoo impressed upon the President that the Bryan ban on loans stood in the way of continued prosperity. "Great prosperity is coming," wrote McAdoo, August 21, 1915. "It will be tremendously increased if we can extend reasonable credits to our customers. . . . To maintain our prosperity we must finance it. Otherwise it may stop and that would be disastrous." Two weeks later Counselor Lansing added his voice:

> If European countries cannot find means to pay . . . they will have to stop buying, and our present export trade will shrink proportionately. The result would be restriction of outputs, industrial depression, idle capital and idle labor, numerous failures, financial demoralization and general unrest and suffering among the laboring classes. . . . Can we afford to let a declaration as to our conception of "the true spirit of neutrality" stand in the way of our national interests, which seem to be seriously threatened?

The ban on loans was accordingly lifted, and the purchases and the prosperity went on. It is easy to conjecture how Wilson could have justified his action to himself. Let Allied purchases stop, let a crash come, let unemployment and discontent stalk the land, let the people turn his administration out in 1916 and restore to power a [Republican] party that had such men as [Theodore] Roosevelt and [Senator Henry Cabot] Lodge high in its counsels—and what chance then would there be for peace or world leadership on a disinterested and elevated plane? No, the best course of action would be to keep the American people busy and prosperous at their peaceful wartime pursuit, the manufacture of munitions.

German Submarines and Wilsonian Legalism

After American supplies had been flowing to England and France for six months, the German government announced, February 4, 1915, that it would attempt to destroy all enemy ships within a stated war zone around the British isles. The submarine was the effective German weapon on the high seas, and Wilson's quixotic position toward this novel means of warfare led to a long train of controversy. A frail craft, extremely vulnerable to the deck guns of armed merchant vessels, the submarine could not be used for the sanctioned practice of visit and search. Since many British merchantmen were armed, the U-boats, to be effective at all, had to remain submerged and rely on hit-and-run war-fare, which meant that there would be no way of providing for the safety of those aboard enemy vessels. This was the German answer to the British blockade, which was intended to starve out the German civilian population. The U-boat retaliation, although less inhumane, was more spectacular. The sinking of the [British passenger liner] *Lusitania* in the spring of 1915 confirmed the growing impression in America that the Germans were monsters. Neither the administration nor the public was much impressed by the Germans' standing offer to relax their methods of submarine warfare if the British would end their blockade on food.

In the face of this situation Wilson continued to allow armed Allied merchant vessels to clear American ports. He further insisted, in spite of strong opposition in Congress, on asserting the right of Americans to travel on belligerent merchant ships in the war zone. When this stand was challenged in the Senate, he declared in a letter to Senator [William J.] Stone:

> I cannot consent to any abridgement of the rights of American citizens in any respect. . . . Once accept a single abatement of right, and many other humiliations would certainly follow, and the whole fine fabric of international law might crumble under our hands piece by piece. What we are contending for in this matter is of the very essence of the things that have made America a sovereign nation.

This was rationalization of the flimsiest sort, for Wilson continued to accept a great deal more than "a single abatement of right" at the hands of the British without the same concern for the effect upon "the whole fine fabric of international law." In dealing with the Allies he made expediency the dominant consideration; in dealing with the Germans, an extremely forward [tough] defense of technical rights—a discrimination for which he and Lansing offered the excuse that British misdeeds involved only property rights whereas German actions involved human rights and took human lives. But Representative Claude Kitchin was among those who pointed out that if Americans would sacrifice their "right" to go on belligerent ships in the submarine zone as readily as they had sacrificed their equal "right" to try to force Britain's "illegal" North Sea mine zone, Germany would not have been guilty of taking American lives. If Wilson's legal dialectics appeared singularly weak, it was because he was forced to find legal reasons for policies that were based not upon law but upon the balance of power and economic necessities.

Peace Rhetoric and Wilson's Re-election

Under the stress of a series of irritations, Wilson seems to have veered toward war with Germany in the spring of 1916; during the winter and spring he delivered a number of emphatic speeches calling for a preparedness program. But in reply to a virtual ultimatum threatening severance of diplomatic relations, the German government at last, on May 4, 1916, gave a satisfactory pledge: henceforth submarine warfare would be conducted in accordance with American demands. For nine months the submarine controversy subsided. At the Democratic national convention a Wilson orator brought rousing cheers with the boast that Wilson, without shedding one drop of blood, had "wrung from the most militant spirit that ever brooded over a battlefield the concession of American demands and American rights." But this concession had been won by a virtual threat of war, and Wilson had placed himself in a position that would require a declaration of war if the pledge should be withdrawn. . . .

In one instant Wilson reaped the whirlwind of unneutrality that he had sown in the first two years of the war.

Like every president before him, Wilson hoped and worked for re-election. The 1916 campaign slogan: "He kept us out of war," was not of his devising; in fact, it frightened him. He seems to have developed a rather exaggerated sense of his powerlessness to live up to such a commitment. "I can't keep the country out of war," he complained to [Secretary of the Navy] Josephus Daniels, "They talk of me as though I were a god. Any little German lieutenant can put us into the war at any time by some calculated outrage." Since the Republican Party was no longer split, the election was extremely close, but Wilson ran well ahead of the rest of the Democratic ticket. Now secure in office for another four years, with the submarine controversy in temporary abeyance, and the conflict with Britain at a relatively high pitch, he turned increasingly toward neutrality. War seems never to have been farther from his mind than in the winter of 1916–17. Although he had not definitively ruled out the possibility of entering the war, it seems—so far as it is possible to understand him—that he had not reconciled himself to going in if he could see any other recourse consistent with his main objectives.

Wilson's Last Quest for Peace Before U.S. Intervention

Just before Christmas 1916 Wilson sent a note to both belligerents calling upon them to state their peace terms, with the impartial observation that "the objects which the statesmen of the belligerents on both sides have in mind in this war are virtually the same, as stated in general terms to their own people and to the world." On January 22, 1917 he made an address before the Senate in which he analyzed the consequences of a crushing defeat of either side and declared that a lasting peace must be a "peace without victory."

> Victory would mean peace forced upon the loser, a victor's terms imposed upon the vanquished. It would be accepted in humiliation, under duress [threat], at an intolerable sacrifice, and would leave a sting, a resentment, a bitter memory upon which terms of peace would rest, not permanently, but only as upon quicksand. Only a peace between equals can last.

The appeal for terms and the call for "peace without victory" were bitterly resented by the Allies, who had been led to feel that the United States was thoroughly committed to them. Colonel House complained in his diary that the President had lost his "punch," that things were drifting aimlessly, that Wilson now stood for "peace at any price." When he once again brought up the matter of preparedness for war, Wilson said flatly: "There will be no war."

At this juncture notice was received from the German government that submarine warfare would be resumed—and in an unrestricted form, directed against neutral as well as belligerent shipping. In one instant Wilson reaped the whirlwind of unneutrality that he had sown in the first two years of the war. For the Germans, realizing that the United

States was already heavily engaged against them with its productive capacity, and assuming that she could not otherwise intervene effectively before a fatal blow could be struck against the Allies, were calculating on American entrance into the war.

When Tumulty brought to Wilson the Associated Press bulletin bearing the news of Germany's decision, the President turned gray and said in quiet tones: "This means war. The break that we have tried to prevent now seems inevitable." Still Wilson waited, as though hoping for some miraculous turn in events that would relieve him of any further decision. In the meantime the plight of the Allies was pressed upon him. Both belligerents were badly strained, in fact, but it was the case of the Allies that he knew. Russia had undergone the March revolution, and her future effectiveness as an ally was extremely doubtful. Morale in the French army was desperately low. ("If France should cave in before Germany," House warned, "it would be a calamity beyond reckoning.") The submarine war would soon constitute a dire threat to England's supply line and bring her to the brink of starvation. Not least, the Allies, their credit facilities exhausted, were facing an economic collapse from which it seemed that nothing short of American participation could save them. This situation [Ambassador to Britain Walter Hines] Page outlined in his famous cablegram to Wilson of March 5: "Perhaps our going to war is the only way in which our preeminent trade position can be maintained and a panic averted. The submarine has added the last item to the danger of a financial world crash." Should Germany win, it appeared, the United States would have the hatred of both victors and vanquished, its influence on the future of Europe and on world peace would be at a minimum, and all the gains of recent years would be lost in an armaments race. Finally, public opinion at home, newly aroused by the revelation of the Zimmermann note,[1] proposing an alliance of Germany, Mexico, and Japan and the annexation of Texas, New Mexico, and Arizona to Mexico, was well prepared for participation. Wilson could not face the consequences, as he saw them, of *not* going to war.

---

1. German foreign secretary Arthur Zimmermann's scheme to draw Mexico into war with the United States if the United States went to war with Germany; the British intercepted the note and revealed its contents to the U.S. government

Wilson's Forebodings About War and Civil Liberties

Still he delayed. Even after German attacks on American ships had begun, Lansing came away from him feeling "that he was resisting the irresistible logic of events." At the end of March, House came to Washington and found him repeating desperately: "What else can I do? Is there anything else I can do?" He told his friend that he did not consider himself fit to be President under wartime conditions. Frank Cobb, of the New York *World*, one of his best friends among the journalists, visiting the sleepless President on the night of April 1, the eve of his war message to Congress, found him still unresolved. Again he asked: "What else can I do? Is there anything else I can do?" Should Germany be defeated, he feared, there would be a dictated peace. There would be no bystanders left with enough power to moderate the terms. "There won't be any peace standards left to work with." As Cobb remembered it:

> W.W. was uncanny that night. He had the whole panorama in his mind. . . .
>
> He began to talk about the consequences to the United States. He had no illusions about the fashion in which we were likely to fight the war.
>
> He said when a war got going it was just war and there weren't two kinds of it. It required illiberalism at home to reinforce the men at the front. We couldn't fight Germany and maintain the ideals of Government that all thinking men shared. He said we would try it but it would be too much for us.
>
> "Once lead this people into war," he said "and they'll forget there ever was such a thing as tolerance. To fight you must be brutal and ruthless, and the spirit of ruthless brutality will enter into the very fibre of our national life, infecting Congress, the courts, the policeman on the beat, the man in the street.". . .
>
> He thought the Constitution would not survive it; that free speech and the right of assembly would go. He said a nation couldn't put its strength into a war and keep its head level; it had never been done.

"If there is any alternative, for God's sake, let's take it," he exclaimed.

But Wilson's war message lay on his desk as he spoke to Cobb, and on the following day he read it to Congress. "It is a fearful thing," he confessed, "to lead this great, peaceful people into war, into the most terrible and disastrous of all wars. . . ." But "the right is more precious than peace." Without rancor [hate], without a single selfish interest, the United States would fight for the principles she had always cherished—"for democracy, for the right of those who submit to authority to have a voice in their own Governments, for the rights and liberties of small nations, for a universal dominion of right by such a concert of free peoples as shall bring peace and safety to all nations and make the world itself at last free."

Woodrow Wilson had changed his means before, but in accepting war he was forced for the first time to turn his back upon his deepest values. The man who had said that peace is the healing and elevating influence of the world was now pledged to use "Force, Force to the utmost, Force without stint or limit." Having given the nation into the hands of a power in which he did not believe, he was now driven more desperately than ever in his life to justify himself, and the rest of his public career became a quest for self-vindication. Nothing less than the final victory of the forces of democracy and peace could wash away his sense of defeat—and Wilson was conscious of defeat in the very hour in which he delivered his ringing war message in tones of such confident righteousness. Returning from the Capitol with the applause of Congress and the people still echoing in his ears, he turned to Tumulty and said: "My message today was a message of death for our young men. How strange it seems to applaud that."

2

American Policy Under Wilson Was Neutral

Arthur S. Link

The late American historian Arthur S. Link ranks as the leading scholar of Woodrow Wilson's career. He not only published a five-volume history of Wilson's presidency until 1917 but also edited more than fifty volumes of Wilson's papers. In the following selection, Link offers a spirited defense of Wilson's adherence to the path of neutrality in the early months of World War I. According to Link, Wilson lived up to his own injunction to the American people at the start of the war to be neutral in thought as well as action. The author does concede, however, that the United States's trade with Great Britain and its acquiescence to the British naval blockade led to a de facto Anglo-American alignment. However, Link does not believe these U.S. actions compromised Wilsonian neutrality. As he argues, the rules governing neutral rights and duties under existing international law in 1914 permitted neutral countries to trade freely. Neutrals were not required to challenge a belligerent (like Britain) that controlled the seas. Link concludes that Wilson made sincere efforts to uphold neutrality as international law defined the concept in 1914.

For Woodrow Wilson and the American people, who had a positive disinclination to play the game of power politics, events on the international stage intruded in an ironic if fateful way from 1914 to 1917. By the spring of 1915 the United States was the only great power not directly involved in the war then raging from western Europe

Arthur S. Link, *Wilson the Diplomatist: A Look at His Major Foreign Policies*. Baltimore, MD: The Johns Hopkins Press, 1957.

to the Far East. Desiring only to deal fairly with both sides and to avoid military involvement, the President soon found that neutrality, as well as war, has its perplexities and perils.

The American Public Favors U.S. Neutrality

Among the most pervasive pressures controlling Wilson's decisions throughout the period 1914–1917 were the attitudes and opinions of the American people concerning the war and America's proper relation to it. Few presidents in American history have been more keenly aware of risks that the leader runs when he ceases to speak for the preponderant majority. "The ear of the leader must ring with the voices of the people. He cannot be of the school of the prophets; he must be of the number of those who studiously serve the slow-paced daily need." Thus Wilson had written in 1890; thus he believed and practiced while formulating his policies toward the belligerents in the First World War.

The dominant American sentiment throughout the period of nonintervention can be . . . characterized by the single adjective "neutral."

The dominant American sentiment throughout the period of nonintervention can be summarily characterized by the single adjective "neutral." This is not to say that Americans had no opinions on the merits of the war and the claims of the opposing alliances, or that there were no differences among the popular reactions. It is simply to state the fairly obvious fact that the preponderant majority, whose opinions played a decisive role in shaping Wilson's policies, did not believe that their interests and security were vitally involved in the outcome of the war and desired to avoid participation if that were possible without sacrificing rights that should not be yielded. The prevalence and astounding vitality of neutralism, in spite of the severest provocations and all the efforts of propagandists on both sides, formed at once the unifying principle of American politics and the compelling reality with which Wilson had to deal from 1914 to 1917.

On the other hand, it would be a large error to imply that Wilson was a prisoner of the public opinion of the majority, and that his will to adopt sterner policies toward one group of belligerents or the other was paralyzed by the stronger counterforce of neutralism. Actually, the evidence points overwhelmingly to the conclusion that Wilson personally shared the opinions of the majority, in brief, that he was substantially neutral in attitude, and that his policies were controlled as much by his own convictions as by the obvious wishes of the people.

Wilson's View of the War

Never once throughout the period of American neutrality did Wilson explain by word of mouth or set down in writing his personal views on the causes and merits of the war. However, this does not mean that one is entirely helpless in trying to reconstruct his methods of thinking and the character of his thought about this subject. There is some direct and considerably more circumstantial evidence to indicate that he set up certain general principles and assumptions at the outset and reasoned deductively from them to form his conclusions.

One of these assumptions was Wilson's belief that the causes of the war were enormously complex and obscure. The conflict, he believed, had its origins in the divisive nationalisms of the Austro-Hungarian Empire, in Russia's drive for free access to the Mediterranean [Sea] in France's longing for the recovery of Alsace-Lorraine [province France lost to Germany in 1870], in Germany's challenge to Britain's naval and commercial supremacy, in the system of rival alliances that had grown up following the Franco-Prussian War [of 1870], and in the general imperialistic rivalries of the late nineteenth and early twentieth centuries. At no time in correspondence or conversation did he ever say, "These are the important root causes of the war." Nevertheless, he revealed conclusively that he thought that they were when he first singled them out as prime causes of international conflict that would have to be removed if the world were ever to achieve a lasting peace.

It followed in Wilson's mind, then, that all the belligerents shared to some degree in the responsibility for the war and that one could not ascribe all blame to one side or the other. Nor could one use simple explanations in talking about conflicting war objectives. It was clear to Wilson that all the belligerents sincerely believed that they were fighting for their existence, but that all of them desired a smashing victory in order to enhance their power, win new territory, and impose crushing indemnities upon their enemies. Because this was true, Wilson reasoned, the best kind of settlement would be a stalemate in which neither alliance would have the power to impose terms upon the other.

Wilson struggled hard and on the whole successfully to be impartial in thought as well as in deed, as he had asked the American people at the outbreak of the war to do.

In his fundamental thinking about war in general, moreover, Wilson shared in a remarkable way the assumptions of the majority of Americans. Like most of his fellow-citizens, he abhorred the very thought of using violence to achieve national objectives; indeed, he was reluctant to use even the threat of force in diplomacy. Like the Socialists, independent radicals, and a large majority of southern and western farmers, he suspected that the financiers and industrialists favored [military] preparedness and a strong foreign policy in order to increase profits and provoke a war that would end the [Progressive] reform movement at home. Like the majority of Americans, he was willing to think of fighting only as a last resort and then only as a means of defending rights that no civilized nation could yield.

Wilson Holds to a Neutral Course

Fortified by these convictions, Wilson struggled hard and on the whole successfully to be impartial in thought as well as in deed, as he had asked the American people at the outbreak of the war to do. In fact, he succeeded in this impossible undertaking far better than most of his contemporaries and his historical critics. His method was to rely upon the general assumptions that he was sure were sound and then virtually to seal himself off from the passionate arguments and indictments of partisans of either alliance, by simply refusing to listen to them. "I recall," Secretary [of State Robert] Lansing afterward wrote, for example, "that . . . his attitude toward evidence of German atrocities in Belgium and toward accounts of the horrors of submarine warfare . . . [was that] he would not read of them and showed anger if the details were called to his attention."

This does not mean that Wilson was able completely to subordinate emotional reactions and personal feelings. Like the majority of Americans, he was to a degree pro-British; on two, perhaps three, occasions during the two and a half years of American neutrality he avowed to close friends his personal sympathy for the Allied cause. But it would be a difficult task to prove that Wilson's pro-British sympathies were ever controlling or indeed even very strong. At no time did he act like a man willing to take measures merely to help his supposed friends. On the contrary, all his policies were aimed either at averting American participation on Britain's side or at ending the war on terms that would have denied the spoils of victory to Britain and her allies. If this is too big an assertion to be taken on faith, then perhaps the reasons for making it will become apparent as we see the way in which Wilson executed policies toward the two leading antagonists.

All authorities, whether friendly or hostile to Wilson, would agree that the acid tests of his neutrality were the policies that he worked out and applied vis-à-vis the British from 1914 to 1917. He has been most condemned by that group of historians highly censorious of his policies, generally known as revisionists, on this score—for becoming the captive of pro-Allied influences within his administration, for condoning such sweeping British control of neutral commerce that the Germans were forced to resort to drastic countermeasures, for permitting American prosperity to become dependent upon loans and exports to the Allies, in short, for permitting a situation to develop that made it inevitable that the United States would go to war if the success of Allied arms was ever seriously threatened.

Like most fallacious arguments, this one contains a certain element of plausibility. Wilson did condone a far-reaching British maritime system. American neutrality did work greatly to the benefit of the Allies. The error arises in saying that these things occurred because Wilson and his advisers necessarily wanted them to occur.

The U.S. Response to the British Maritime System

Perhaps the best way to gain a clear understanding of why Anglo-American relations developed as they did from 1914 to 1917 is to see how the policies that decisively shaped those relations emerged in several stages in response to certain pressures, events, and forces. The first stage, lasting from August, 1914, to about August, 1915, was in many ways the most critical, because the basic American response to the war and to the British maritime system was formulated then. That response was governed in the first instance by two domestic realities: the overwhelming, virtually unanimous, American desire to be neutral, and the pressures in the United States for a large measure of free trade with Britain's enemies.

In view of the prevailing American sentiment at the outbreak of the war, a policy of strict official neutrality was the only possible course for the United States government. This fact prompted the President's official proclamations of neutrality, supplemented by his appeal to the American people for impartiality in thought. . . .

One cannot read the records revealing how these policies were formulated without being convinced that their authors were high-minded in their determination to be fair to both sides. Indeed, Wilson and the man who chiefly influenced him in the formulation of the rules of neutrality, Secretary of State [William Jennings] Bryan, were so intent upon being fair to the Germans that they adopted policies during the first months of the war that were highly disadvantageous to the British, if not unneutral. One was to prevent the sale of submarine parts, and hence parts for any naval craft, by a private American firm to the British government, on the ground that such a sale would be "contrary to . . . strict neutrality." Wilson persisted in supporting Bryan in this matter, in spite of advice from Counselor [Robert] Lansing and the Joint Neutrality Board to the effect that their position was contrary to international law.

Loans and Blockades

Infinitely more damaging to the Allies was the administration's second effort to lean over backward in being "strictly" neutral—the ban of loans by American bankers to the belligerent governments that the President permitted Bryan to impose in August, 1914. From a technical viewpoint, the ban was not unneutral, but it was highly prejudicial to the Allies because its effect was potentially to deny them their otherwise legal right to purchase supplies in the American market. These two incidents are not to be understood as revealing any anti-British bias on the part of Wilson and Bryan, although British officials at the time were convinced that they did. I mention them only to show what an important role the administration's desire to be impartial played in the formation of policies vis-à-vis the British during the early period of American neutrality.

American neutrality did work greatly to the benefit of the Allies.

The other pressure shaping American policies at this time was the force of combined demands at home for the virtually free transit of American ships and goods to the European neutrals and the belligerent Central Powers. So powerful were these demands, especially from Cottson growers and exporters and their spokesmen in Congress, that Wilson personally sponsored two measures highly disadvantageous to the British and unneutral in fact as well as in spirit. One was a change in the ship registry law, put into effect by an act approved August 18, 1914, which made it easy for German or other foreign shipping firms to take out American registry for their vessels. The other was a plan to establish a federal corporation to purchase German ships in American ports and to use them to carry supplies to the belligerents, particularly to Germany. Wilson applied heavy pressure to obtain congressional approval of this, the so-called ship-purchase bill, during the short term from December, 1914, to March, 1915; he failed only because of a stout senatorial filibuster.

In negotiations with the British government during the early months of the war, Wilson fought hard in response to domestic pressures to keep the channels of international commerce open to American ships and goods. He did not go as far in defense of neutral rights as some of his predecessors, but he did suggest a code so sweeping that an enforcement of it would have meant almost total destruction of the British system of maritime controls. Specifically, the President first proposed on August 6, 1914, that the belligerents adopt the rules of naval warfare laid down in the Declaration of London of 1909, a convention never ratified by Great Britain or the United States, which permitted the free transit of all goods except those obviously contraband. When the British rejected this suggestion, the President came back on October 16, proposing a compromise that would have still seriously impaired the effectiveness of British sea power. When this effort also failed, Wilson then announced that his government would assert and defend all its rights under international law and treaties.

I have described these policies and proposals because they so clearly reveal Wilson's neutral intentions and what he would have done in matters of trade had he been able to make the rules himself. But he obviously could not follow his personal preferences alone or respond only to domestic pressures. In seeking to assert and defend American neutral rights he ran head-on into a reality as important as the reality of the pressures at home. It was the British determination to use sea power to prevent American ships and goods from going to the sustenance of the German economy and military forces.

British assumption of a nearly absolute control of the seas washing western Europe began with relatively mild measures in August, 1914, and culminated in the suppression of virtually all commerce to the Central Powers in March, 1915. For the British, this was not a question of adhering to the laws of blockade or of violating them, or of doing things merely to be nice to American friends. It was a question of achieving their supreme objective, to deprive their enemies of vital raw materials and goods, without risking the alienation of the United States. The controlling fact for the British was the necessity of preserving American friendship, in order to assure the uninterrupted rhythm of the North Atlantic trade. . . .

Why the United States Yielded to the British Blockade

The crucial question all along . . . was whether the United States, the only neutral power strong enough successfully to challenge the British measures, would acquiesce or resist to the point of threatening or using force. The American response during the formative period of neutrality was, in brief, to accept the British system and to limit action against it to a vigorous assertion of American legal rights for future adjudication. All this is too well known to require any further exposition. What is not so well understood are the reasons why Wilson and his advisers acquiesced in a solution that denied the objectives that they and a large segment of the American public demanded. These reasons may be briefly summarized, as follows:

First, the British maritime system, in spite of American allegations to the contrary, enjoyed the advantage of being legitimate and usually legal, or nearly so, by traditional criteria. It was legitimate rather than fraudulent, and legal rather than capricious or terroristic, in its major aspects because the British did in fact hold undisputed sea supremacy and were therefore able to execute their controls in an orderly fashion. In asserting their own rights, the Americans could not well deny the advantages that accrued to the British by virtue of their sea power. The British, for example, had an undoubted right to establish a blockade of the Central Powers, and the American attempt to persuade the London government to use techniques effective only in the days of the sailing ship did not have much cogency in the twentieth century.

Wilson's refusal to challenge the British maritime system, in short, to break the British blockade, was almost inevitable.

Second, much of the success of the British in establishing their control depended upon the way in which they went about it. Had they instituted their total blockade at the outset of the war, the American reaction would undoubtedly have been violent. Instead, the British applied their controls gradually, with a careful eye upon American opinion, using the opportunities provided by recurrent crises in German-American relations to institute their severest measures.

Third, the British were careful never to offend so many American interests at one time that retaliation would have been inevitable, or any single interest powerful enough by itself to compel retaliation. There was the case of cotton, which the officials in London were determined to prevent from going to Germany because it was an ingredient of gunpowder. Not until a year after the war began did they put cotton on the list of absolute contraband; even then they went to the extraordinary length of underwriting the entire

American cotton market in order to avert an irresistible southern pressure in Congress for retaliation. In addition, although they were ruthless in enforcing their blockade, the British took careful pains to avoid any serious injury to American property interests. They confiscated only the most obvious contraband; in all doubtful cases they paid value for cargoes or ships seized. Their objective was to control, not to destroy, American commerce.

Fourth, there was great significance in the language and symbolism that the British Foreign Office used in defending the measures of the [British] Admiralty and Ministry of Blockade. By justifying their maritime system in terms of international law and the right of retaliation, and (at least before the summer of 1916) by making an honest effort to meet American objections half way when possible, the British made it almost inevitable that the Washington authorities would have to reply in the same language, thus giving a purely *legal* character to the issues of sovereignty and inherent national rights. The significance of this achievement can be seen in the conviction of Wilson and the majority of Americans that the Anglo-American disputes did involve only property rights, which should be vindicated only by an appeal to much-controverted [much-debated] international law. Moreover, by appealing to the American government and people in the name of friendship and by always professing their devotion to the cause of humanity, the British succeeded in evoking strong feelings of sympathy and understanding on the other side of the water.

Finally, the British were able partially to justify their own blockade measures as legitimate adaptations to a changing technology by pointing to precedents established by the Washington government itself during the American Civil War. . . . Their main contention—that the American government had also stretched the rules of blockade to allow for technological changes—was essentially correct.

Wilson's Wise Leadership

Wilson's refusal to challenge the British maritime system, in short, to break the British blockade, was almost inevitable in view of the facts we have just reviewed, *if the President's objective was simply to maintain as best he could the neutral position of the United States.* An absolute neutrality was in any event impossible because of the total character of the war and

America's importance in the world economy. It often happened that any action by the United States inevitably conferred a benefit on one side and thereby injured the other, at least indirectly. In these circumstances, neutrality often consisted of doing the things that would give the least unwarranted or undeserved advantages.

By this standard, it would have been more unneutral than neutral for Wilson to have broken the British maritime system by enforcing highly doubtful technical rights under international law. Judged by practical standards rather than by the often conflicting criteria of neutrality, Wilson's acceptance of the British system seems realistic and wise—indeed, the only choice that he could have made in the circumstances. This is true because the results of destroying the British blockade would have been the wrecking of American friendship with the two great European democracies [Great Britain and France] and the probable victory of the Central Powers, without a single compensating gain for the interests and security of the United States. Only the sure achievement of some great political objective like a secure peace settlement, certainly not the winning of a commercial advantage or the defense of doubtful neutral rights, would have justified Wilson in undertaking a determined challenge to British sea power.

3

The Sinking of the *Lusitania* Was a Criminal German Action

The Outlook

The torpedoing of the British passenger liner *Lusitania* on May 7, 1915, off the Irish coast by a German submarine, the U-20, was a turning point on the American road to intervention in the Great War. Over eleven hundred people, including 128 Americans, drowned in the disaster. The event stemmed from Germany's decision in early 1915 to impose a submarine blockade of the British Isles in retaliation for Britain's severe maritime blockade of Germany. The *Lusitania* was carrying munitions of war and other contraband from the United States to Britain, and Germany had publicly warned Americans against sailing such vessels into the submarine zone. However, the unarmed ship was clearly a passenger vessel protected by international maritime rules forbidding surprise submarine attack. American political leaders and newspapers passionately denounced the German attack. President Woodrow Wilson demanded that Germany make reparations and disavow the sinking. However, few Americans as yet called for war. The following 1915 editorial from the *Outlook*, a New York weekly magazine, assails the sinking as a criminal act requiring a tough American response. The *Outlook* calls for a German apology and pledge to stop submarine attacks on merchant vessels in the future. The *Outlook* editors applaud President Wilson's quick and strong response to Germany. They also provide an account of the day the *Lusitania* sank and condemn Germany's "might makes right" justification for its actions.

"The *Lusitania* Massacre," *The Outlook*, May 19, 1915, pp. 103–107.

The sinking of the Lusitania was not an act of war, it was a crime—the crime of murder. "War is a public armed contest between nations, under the sanction of international law, to establish justice between them." In the sinking of the Lusitania there was no armed contest, and the fundamental moralities of international law were violated. War is cruel; but it is not lawless. It is killing; but it is not murder. No such wholesale massacre of unarmed and defenseless victims has been perpetrated in modern warfare since [Napoléon], Bonaparte's massacre of defenseless prisoners on the shore of the Mediterranean Sea at Jaffa.

America Must Answer German Aggressions

Has America any duty to disown this crime against itself, against the civilized world, against humanity?. . .

We have seen the neutrality of weak nations violated, private property destroyed, defenseless cities bombarded, churches and hospitals, which civilized warfare has always regarded as sacred, demolished, and have said nothing. We have seen one American ship on the high seas bombarded from the air, and another torpedoed from the sea, and have declared that if another American life is lost we shall call the assailant to "a strict accountability." Now over a hundred American lives are lost. What shall we do? What ought we to do?

Does America owe any duty of protection to its citizens in foreign lands and on the high seas? Patient waiting has done nothing. Protesting words have done nothing. In the presence of wholesale assassination The Outlook is not neutral. We believe the time has come for National action. In such a crisis courage is a duty and timidity a crime.

The sinking of the Lusitania was not an act of war, it was a crime—the crime of murder.

We need not wait for official investigation. The murder is exultantly avowed. We need not wait for judicial investigation of the defenses offered. The War Zone? No nation has a right to put an invisible fence around a section of the open sea and warn all neutral nations off as trespassers, at the peril of their lives. Warning given? When did warning of an intent to commit murder serve as an excuse for the murder perpetrated? The Lusitania was armed? She was not armed; but she had a right to be. The Constitution of the United States recognizes the right of peaceable citizens to bear arms; international law recognizes to a similar reasonable degree the right of peaceable vessels to bear arms. She was carrying contraband? Then she might be sunk; but not until the safety of her crew and passengers was assured. Great Britain is starving Germany, therefore Germany has a right to murder American citizens? A strange logic! But Great Britain is not starving Germany. The laws of war forbid the murder of the unarmed, but they also declare in explicit terms that "it is lawful to starve a hostile belligerent, armed or unarmed, so that it leads to the speedier subjection of the enemy." The invention of air-ships and submarines has changed international law? [American lawyer and international law expert] John Bassett Moore is our authority for saying that it has not changed international law. Certainly it has not changed the Ten Commandments. The use of a novel instrument does not change the nature of the crime. Murder is still murder; and killing unarmed noncombatants in cold blood the conscience of all civilized nations still condemns as murder.

U.S. Countermeasures
Needed Against Germany

The time for words has passed; the time for National action has come. What action? Any action which vigorously and effectively disowns all fellowship with a nation which commits wholesale piracy on the high seas. The action which we hope will have been taken by the United States Government before this number reaches our readers is this:

We would have our Government at once call upon Germany to disown and repudiate her present practice of sinking merchant vessels without warning and without regard for safety of passengers and crew, and notify Germany that so long as she continues to disregard the rights of neutrals and the fundamental principles of humanity the United States will have no intercourse with her. We would have our Government give the German Ambassador his passport and call home from Germany the American Ambassador. We would publicly request by cable all the neutral Powers of the world to unite with us in this action; if they decline, we would still take the action alone.

This does not mean war against Germany.

But if, as a result, Germany declared war against us, we would have America meet the peril with the same spirit of courage with which our fathers met a greater peril in 1776 and in 1812. To this action there are objections. There are objections to any action. But there are still greater objections to inaction, for inaction means America's acquiescence in Germany's continuing policy of international crime.

The Lusitania was not armed, and never has been, but she did carry in her cargo munitions of war and other contraband.

We do not know the individual who is responsible for this piracy on the high seas. Not the German people. It is not their act. Germany is not a republic. Her Government is not responsible to her people. They have not directed its policy. They could not change it if they would; they cannot even give free expression to their opinions respecting it. Speech and press are free in America; they are free in England; they are not free in Germany. And where opinions cannot be freely expressed public opinion does not exist. It is created by expression. This piracy should stir no hate against the German people—only compassion and a new hope that they may become free.

It is not for us to judge even the director of these acts of barbaric brutality—whoever he may be. He will be self-judged. The time will come when will pass away the burning fever of war which now blinds the eyes and hardens the heart, and the ghosts of his murdered victims, innocent of wrong, will surround with their accusing voices this now exultant assassin. . . .

Support for Wilson's Ultimatum to Germany

The Outlook Office, Friday Morning, May 14.

The foregoing editorial went to press yesterday morning. We stop the press to say that the President's message to the Imperial German Government is published this morning. The country has looked forward to it with mingled feelings of eagerness, anxiety, and confidence. Every patriotic American will greet it with hearty approval and satisfaction.

In accordance with diplomatic conventions it is signed by the Secretary of State, but manifestly it is written by the hand of the President himself. For style, spirit, courtesy, vigor, and the principles it expresses, it will take a high place among the state papers of our Government.

The President narrates the series of violations of American rights which culminated in the sinking of the Lusitania; assumes that "these acts, so absolutely contrary to the rules, the practices, and the spirit of modern warfare," are not approved by the Imperial German Government; asserts that Americans have the right to travel on merchant ships even when these ships are owned by belligerents; states as undebatable the fact that submarine warfare against merchant ships violates "many sacred principles of justice and humanity;" informs the Imperial German Government that the German Embassy at Washington printed a warning to the people of the United States in a newspaper advertisement, which was not only an act of diplomatic discourtesy, but which cannot possibly "be accepted as an excuse or palliation [appeasement]" for the death-dealing destruction of the Lusitania; takes it for granted that the commanders of the submarines who have torpedoed non-combatants acted "under a misapprehension of the orders" of the Imperial German Government; expresses the confident expectation that the Imperial German Government will make reparation, in so far as reparation for injuries which cannot be measured may be made, and will immediately take steps to prevent the recurrence of such injuries; and, finally . . . states the intention of the Government of the United States to support its demands for justice by acting, if action is necessary. . . .

The President's ultimatum is the first step. . . . He has cleared the atmosphere and made the issue plain.

Every loyal American should support the President in his hope that Germany will accede to his just demands.

But if, unhappily, Germany decides against us, every loyal American, whatever his ancestry or his place of birth, should be *preparing now* to omit no act necessary to the performance of his sacred duty of aiding the Government of the United States to protect its citizens. . . .

The Evidence of the "Crime"

On Monday of last week [May 10] a British coroner's jury, in their finding on deaths caused by the sinking of the Cunard steamship Lusitania, declared: "The jury finds this appalling crime was contrary to international law and the conventions of all civilized nations, and we therefore charge the officers of the submarine and the German Emperor and the Government of Germany, under whose orders they acted, with the crime of willful and wholesale murder."

What was this crime, thus characterized?

On the first day of May the Lusitania left New York City bound for Queenstown [Ireland] and Liverpool. Built eight years ago at a cost of seven and a half million dollars, she was one of the Cunard Line's famous trio of the largest, finest, and fastest British ships afloat—the Lusitania, Mauretania, and Aquitania. Aboard her were over two thousand men, women, and children. The day before she sailed the German Embassy issued a printed warning to Americans to the effect that if they sailed the high seas on British passenger ships they did so at the peril of their lives. It is said that individuals received also personal warnings in the form of telegrams, but there is doubt about this. Generally, the German warnings were regarded as "bluff," and great faith was put by the passengers in the Lusitania's speed, the belief that British war-ships would protect her, and in the feeling that no nation or ruler would be so dastardly as to destroy human life of neutrals and non-combatants by wholesale for remote military advantage and contrary to fixed principles of international practice. An unusual number of women, and especially children, were on board, many of them going to rejoin their husbands and fathers in England. The Lusitania was not armed, and never has been, but she did carry in her cargo munitions of war and other contraband.

The Lusitania Captain's Account

On Friday, May 7, Captain Turner, of the Lusitania, was on the bridge at two o'clock; many of the passengers were at their luncheon; the ship was running rather slowly—in order, as the captain says, that it might not reach port at a wrong stage of the tide. The Admiralty had by wireless informed Captain Turner of the presence of submarines in the Irish Channel, but had furnished no destroyers or other war-ships to guard the passage—in the House of Commons [First Lord of the Admiralty] Winston Churchill has said that it was impossible so to guard all passenger ships, and it has even been doubted whether the presence of convoys would be a protection or a detriment. Mr. Simon Lake, the American submarine inventor, has declared that their smoke would attract submarines and that there really is no such thing as a submarine defense. In accordance with the Admiralty's directions, the ship was keeping a middle course in the channel. The position of the vessel on its way to Queenstown was off Old Head, Kinsale, ten miles or more from the Irish coast. Suddenly Captain Turner and several others, officers and passengers, saw, half a mile or so away and off the starboard side, the periscope of a submarine. What followed may be described in Captain Turner's words:

Incidents of heroism and coolness were not wanting.

I saw a torpedo speeding toward us, and immediately I tried to change our course, but was unable to maneuver out of its way. There was a terrible impact as the torpedo struck the starboard side of the vessel, and a second torpedo followed almost immediately. This one struck squarely over the boilers.

I tried to turn the Lusitania shoreward, hoping to beach her, but her engines were crippled, and it was impossible.

There has been criticism because I did not order the lifeboats out sooner; but no matter what may be done there are always some to criticise. Until the Lusitania came to a standstill it was absolutely out of the question to launch the boats—they would have been swamped.

To this Captain Turner added: "I saw the torpedoes with my own eyes. It was cold-blooded murder." Some accounts say that the German submarine fired the fatal torpedoes.

The two torpedoes struck without any appreciable lapse of time between them. The ship instantly took a strong list to port, making it impossible to handle the boats on the starboard side. From the time of the attack until the sinking of the ship less than twenty minutes elapsed. There was a rush for life-belts. Some passengers threw off their outer clothing, and thereby helped their chances of floating; others put on heavy coats and furs, and few of these were picked up. Several boats were launched (perhaps ten), but not all successfully.

Queenstown had been informed by wireless, and in time

many steamboats, ships, and tugs arrived and helped in the search for survivors and for bodies of the dead.

Prominent Americans On Board

Incidents of heroism and coolness were not wanting. Thus, one deck steward has received warm praise for the way in which he cheered and captained a boat-load of forlorn and helpless people. Mr. Alfred G. Vanderbilt, of the wealthy and famous family of that name, is described by an onlooker as taking off his life-belt to give to an old lady and as working hard to get children into the boats. He was going to Europe to extend his already large efforts to render ambulance and hospital aid. He was among the lost. Mr. Charles Frohman, the most prominent figure in American theatrical circles, was also lost. He is said to have remarked to a companion: "Why fear death? It is the most beautiful adventure in life." Elbert Hubbard, the well-known writer; Justus M. Forman, novelist and playwright; Charles Klein, the dramatist, whose "Music Master" and other plays are known to every one, were among the Americans of special prominence who were lost.

There was no panic, although there has been some question as to the efficiency of the crew in handling boats and passengers. The time was terribly short and the difficulties of the case almost beyond description. The old Anglo-Saxon cry of "Women and children first" was heard and heeded. One passenger gives the following description of the scene:

> On the decks of the doomed vessel absolute calmness prevailed. There was no rushing about and nothing resembling a panic. In a few isolated cases there were signs of hysteria on the part of women, but that was all. I did not notice any concerted effort to distribute life-belts, and I was unable to obtain one.

The efforts made to lower the boats had not apparently met with much success.

Women were standing quite calmly, waiting for an opportunity to enter the boats when they should be released by the men from the davits.

The same passenger, after telling how he dived from the ship, gives a pen picture of the actual sinking of the Lusitania:

> I turned around to watch the great ship heel over. The

monster took a sudden plunge, and I saw a crowd still on her decks, and boats filled with helpless women and children glued to her side. I sickened with horror at the sight.

There was a thunderous roar, as of the collapse of a great building on fire; then she disappeared, dragging with her hundreds of fellow-creatures into the vortex. Many never rose to the surface, but the sea rapidly grew thick with the figures of struggling men and women and children.

The total toll of the dead as it appears at this writing is 1,150, of whom 114 were known to be American citizens and others to be of long American residence although not citizens. Of the survivors, 465 were passengers, 302 were of the crew. The funeral services at Queenstown were touching and pathetic to the utmost degree.

"The ship was as defenseless against undersea . . . attack as a Hoboken ferryboat in the North River would be against one of the United States battle-ships."

An inquiry is to be made into the tragedy by the British Board of Trade under the leadership of Lord Mersey, who presided over the Titanic inquiry. In the House of Commons the First Lord of the Admiralty, Winston Churchill, said:

I must make it plain that in no circumstances will it be possible to make public the naval dispositions for patrolling our coasts. Our resources do not enable us to provide destroyer escorts for mail and passenger ships. The Admiralty had general knowledge of the German warning issued in America, and from that knowledge and other information concerning submarine movements it sent warnings to the Lusitania and directions as to her course.

Attacked Without Warning

There was absolutely no warning given by the submarine before the attack; after the Lusitania sank a submarine emerged in the middle of the wreck and ruin, its officers surveyed the scene, then the submarine submerged and doubtless fled to its base.

One writer truly says: "The ship was as defenseless against undersea and underhand attack as a Hoboken [city in New Jersey] ferryboat in the North River would be against one of the United States battle-ships."

Germany's "Might Makes Right" Defense

If there were any hope entertained that Germany would repudiate the act of her submarines in destroying the Lusitania and with it many hundreds of lives of non-combatants, many of whom were women and children, that hope was quickly dispelled.

Through the mouth of her non-official representative in this country, Dr. [Bernhard] Dernburg, through the words of the German Ambassador to the United States, through an official statement from Berlin, and in every other possible way Germany has approved the massacre and has sought to give a defense for the act to the world and to history. A triple defense, indeed, is called for: First, toward Great Britain, for the violation of settled international law and the destruction of a British merchant ship without an opportunity to its crew and British subjects for escape; second, to the United States for the deliberate, planned slaughter of American citizens; third, to the world for what is everywhere, except in German circles, regarded as the most terrible attack on human rights to life and safety that the world has known.

The essence of all the defenses put forth by Germany is, to speak plainly, that "might makes right;" German advantage in the war is a necessity, and therefore anything conceivable is justified if German advantage gains. As one writer of the countless letters to the newspapers tersely puts it: "If, on the one hand, you have an indirect military advantage for Germany and, on the other hand, the lives of American citizens—drown the Americans."

4

The Sinking of the *Lusitania* Was Retaliation for Britain's Blockade Strategy

The Fatherland

When the British luxury liner *Lusitania* was torpedoed on May 7, 1915, killing more than one thousand people, including 128 Americans, most American newspapers and magazines bitterly condemned the German action. However, there were pro-German elements in the United States who viewed the event differently. The *Fatherland*, an aggressively pro-German New York weekly read by German Americans, defended German motives and actions in the episode. It blamed the British government, the British-based Cunard Line that owned and operated the ship, and the U.S. government for bringing on the tragedy. American citizens, the *Fatherland* argued, should have been warned by the U.S. government not to travel on belligerent vessels, especially those carrying munitions. The journal also alleged that exploding munitions on the ship contributed to the sinking more than the German torpedoes did. (Few historians accept this contention today, however.) Another contention of the *Fatherland* is that the German submarine weapon was a response to Britain's own harsh naval weapon—the blockade of Germany. This excerpt from the *Fatherland* editorial exemplifies the division of loyalties of Americans at the beginning of the war with German Americans favoring their former homeland and Anglo-Americans lauding

"Why the *Lusitania* Was Sunk," *The Fatherland*, May 19, 1915.

the British cause. American neutrality became more tenuous in the wake of the *Lusitania* crisis.

L ast week [May 1915] we predicted the fate that has overtaken the *Lusitania. The Fatherland* did not reach the news-stands till Saturday, but the editorial in question was written several days before publication. To-day we make another prediction. Every large passenger ship bound for England is practically a swimming arsenal, carrying vast quantities of ammunition and explosives of every description. An arsenal, whether on sea or land, is not a safe place for women and children. It is not a safe place for anyone. Every now and then we read of a warship blown up by an explosion caused by spontaneous combustion, in spite of the rigid care exercised to prevent such an accident. Our passenger ships carry more explosives than the ordinary man-of-war. No innocent passenger should be allowed to embark on a vessel carrying explosives. *It stands to reason that a fate not unlike that of the Lusitania will meet before long a passenger ship by an explosion of vast stores of ammunition within.* While Germany is not bound to respect a flag of any ship carrying implements of murder, German submarines may discriminate in favor of a neutral flag. Spontaneous combustion recognizes no international convention.

Much as we regret the staggering loss of life in the disaster that startled the world, the facts in the case absolutely justify the action of the Germans.

No Basis for Protest

Legally and morally there is no basis for any protest on the part of the United States. The *Lusitania* was a British ship. British ships have been instructed by the Admiralty to ram submarines and to take active measures against the enemy. Hence every British ship must be considered in the light of a warship.

The *Lusitania* flew the ensign of the British Naval Reserves before the submarine warfare was initiated. Since that time she has hoisted many a flag, including the Stars and Stripes. According to a statement issued by the advertising manager of the Cunard Line, the *Lusitania* "when torpedoed was entirely out of the control of the Cunard Company and operated under the command of the British Admiralty."

The *Lusitania* carried contraband [munitions] of war from this country to England. If this contraband had reached its destination it would undoubtedly have killed far more Germans than the total number of passengers lost on the *Lusitania*. As a matter of fact it did actually kill the passengers by precipitating the sinking of the ship. There can be no doubt that the ship would not have sunk for hours, if explosions from within had not hastened its end. *Every passenger on a boat carrying contraband of war takes his life into his hands.* The explosives in the hold of a ship, we repeat, constitutes a graver peril to passengers than the shots of German torpedoes.

Much as we regret the staggering loss of life in the disaster that startled the world, the facts in the case absolutely justify the actions of the Germans.

It cannot be said that the *Lusitania* was torpedoed without warning. Ordinarily a half hour's warning is regarded sufficient. In this case the ship was warned of its fate *four or five days in advance.* We need only turn to the warning notice issued by the German Embassy on the day before the *Lusitania* left the harbor of New York.

Instead of urging the President to take steps against Germany, we should impeach the Secretary of State for his neglect of duty in not warning all Americans of the peril of ocean traffic in the war zone, especially under the flag of a belligerent nation. If the Secretary of State . . . had issued such a warning, not a single American life would have been forfeited.

Germany, provoked by England which established a war zone as early as November [1914] and made the importation of foodstuffs into Germany practically impossible, decided upon submarine warfare as a measure of retaliation. She was forced to do so by the signal failure of the United States to protect the common rights of neutrals. When Germany determines upon a plan of action she means business. The Germans are not a nation of poker players. Germany does not bluff.

The sinking of the *Lusitania* is a terrific lesson, but in order to drive home its force more fully and to safeguard this country from further losses and from the danger of complications with Germany, the State Department should issue at once a formal notice admonishing American citizens to shun all ships flying the flag of a belligerent nation and all ships, *irrespective of nationality*, which carry across the sea the tools of destruction.

The Cunard Line

But if we accuse the State Department of negligence, we should indict the officials of the Cunard Line for murder. They knew that the *Lusitania* was a floating fortress. Yet, for the sake of sordid gain, they jeopardized the lives of more than two thousand people. When the German Embassy issued its warning, the Cunard Line pooh-poohed the danger so as not to forfeit the shekels paid for the passage.

Did the Cunard Line tell its prospective passengers that its crew was short of eighty or ninety stokers?

Did the Cunard Line inform its passengers that the *Lusitania* . . . narrowly escaped an attack by a submarine on a previous voyage?

Did they inform the passengers of the fact that one of its turbines was defective?

How many of the passengers would have remained on the boat if the officials of the Cunard Line had not suppressed the truth?

Those innocent victims believed in the protection of the British Admiralty. The Captain of the *Lusitania* admits that the Admiralty "never seemed to bother" about the *Lusitania*. He knew that England, though she waives the rules, no longer rules the waves. He is a soldier under orders of the Admiralty. He has a right to take chances with his own life. But what right has he to take chances with the lives of his crew and his two thousand passengers?

Chapter 2

American Military Preparedness

1

America Needs
Military Preparedness

Leonard Wood

General Leonard Wood (1860–1927) had a remarkable career that, at various stages, saw him fight against Apache Indian chief Geronimo, serve with his friend Theodore Roosevelt in the Rough Riders during the Spanish-American War, and become a successful military governor of Cuba after that conflict. Before World War I, he also served as army chief of staff. In the following excerpt from a 1916 essay, Wood makes the case for a vigorous American program of military preparedness in light of the world war. He warns that the United States must be ready to defend itself or risk losing its sovereignty. Wood viewed preparedness not just as a buildup of weaponry but also as a means of forging national unity in an America marked by serious social divisions. Wood also backs universal military service for American men. He was convinced that America's historic reliance on volunteer soldiers in time of war was grossly inadequate to the present danger and that the United States must make some kind of military service obligatory.

What lesson will America draw from the present Great War? Must she see the heads of her own children at the foot of the guillotine to realize that it will cut, or will she accept the evidence of the thousands which have lain there before? Will she heed the lesson of all time, that national unpreparedness means national downfall, or will she profit from the experience and misfortunes of others and take those needed measures of preparedness which prudence and

Leonard Wood, "What the War Means to America," *The Story of the Great War*, vol. 1, edited by Francis J. Reynolds et al. New York: P.F. Collier & Son, 1916.

wisdom dictate. In a word, will she draw any valuable lessons from the Great War? This is the question which is so often asked. As yet there is no answer.

The Case for Military Readiness

It is the question uppermost in the minds of all those who are intelligently interested in our country's welfare and safety. It is the question which vitally concerns all of us, as it concerns the defense and possibly the very existence of our nation. The answer must be "Preparedness." If we are to live, preparedness to oppose the force of wrong with the strength of right. Will it be? That's the question! Or will America drift on blind to the lessons of the world tragedy, heedless of consequences, concerned with the accumulation of wealth, satiated with a sense of moral worth which the world does not so fully recognize, planning to capture the commerce of the warring nations, and expecting at the same time to retain their friendship and regard. Let us hope that, in the light of what is, and as a preparation against what may be, the answer will be characteristic of a great people, peaceful, but prudent and foreseeing; that it will be thorough, carefully thought-out preparedness; preparedness against war. A preparedness which if it is to be lasting and secure must be founded upon the moral organization of our people; an organization which will create and keep alive in the heart of every citizen a sense not only of obligation for service to the nation in time of war or trouble, but also of obligation to so prepare himself as to render this service effective. An organization which will recognize that the basic principle upon which a free democracy or representative government rests, and must rest, if they are to survive the day of stress and trouble, is, that with manhood suffrage goes manhood obligation for service, not necessarily with arms in hand, but for service somewhere in that great complex mass which constitutes the organization of a nation's might and resources for defense; organization which will make us think in terms of the nation and not those of city, State, or personal interest; organization which will result in all performing service for the nation with singleness of purpose in a common cause—preparedness for defense: preparedness to discharge our plain duty whatever it may be. Such service will make for national solidarity, the doing away with petty distinctions of class and creed, and fuse the various elements of this people into one homogeneous mass of real Americans, and leave us a better and a stronger people.

Will she [the United States] heed the lesson of all time, that national unpreparedness means national downfall?

Once such a moral organization is accomplished, the remaining organization will be simple. This will include an organization of transportation, on land and sea, and of communications. An organization of the nation's industrial resources so that the energy of its great manufacturing plants may be promptly turned into making what they can best make to supply the military needs of the nation. By military needs we mean all the complex requirements of a nation engaged in war, requirements which are, many of them, requirements of peace as well as of war. It will also include a thorough organization of the country's chemical resources and the development thereof, so that we may be as little dependent as possible upon materials from oversea. At present many important and essential elements come from over-sea nations and would not be available in case of loss of sea control. We must devise substitutes or find means of making these things. Chemistry is one of the great weapons of modern war. There must also be organization which will provide a regular army organized on sound lines, supplied with ample reserves of men and material; an army adequate to the peace needs of the nation, which means, among other things, the secure garrisoning of our oversea possessions, including the Philippines and the Hawaiian Islands. These latter are the key to the Pacific, and one of the main defenses of the Pacific Coast and of the Panama Canal. Whoever holds these islands will dominate the trade routes of the Pacific, and in a large measure the Pacific itself.

The Value of a Strong Army and Navy

The regular army should also be sufficient for the secure holding and safeguarding of the Panama Canal, an instrument of war of the greatest importance, so long as it is in our control, greatly increasing the value of our navy, and an implement of commerce of tremendous value, a possession so valuable and of such vital importance to us that we cannot allow it to lie outside our secure grasp.

It must also be adequate to provide garrisons in Porto Rico and Alaska, and at the same time maintain in the continental United States a force of coast artillery sufficient to furnish the necessary manning details for our seacoast defenses, and a mobile force complete in every detail and adequate in time of war to meet the first shock of an invasion and sufficient in time of peace to meet the various demands made upon it for home service, such as troops for home emergencies or disorders, troops for the necessary training of the National Militia, also sufficient officers and noncommissioned officers for duty at schools, colleges, military training camps and in various other capacities. It must be also strong enough to provide a strong expeditionary force, such as we sent to Cuba in 1898, without interfering with its regular duties.

The necessity of building and maintaining an adequate navy, well balanced, thoroughly equipped and maintained at the highest standard of efficiency and ready always for immediate service, with necessary adjuncts afloat and ashore, is also one of the clear lessons of the war; others are the establishment of ammunition plants at points sufficiently remote from the seacoast, and so placed as to render their capture and destruction improbable in case of sudden invasion; the provision of an adequate reserve corps of 50,000 officers, a number sufficient for one and one-half million of citizen soldiers; officers well trained and ready for immediate service; the provision of adequate supplies and reserve supplies of artillery, arms, and ammunition of all types for these troops.

The great outstanding lesson of the war is that we must not trust to righteousness and fair dealing alone.

We must also build up a system under which officers and men for our citizen soldiery can be trained with the minimum of interference with their educational or industrial careers, under conditions which will permit the accomplishment of their training during the period of youth, and once this is accomplished will permit their return to their normal occupations with the minimum of delay.

Lessons of the War

The lesson which we should draw from the Great War is that nothing should be left to chance or to the promise of others, or to the fair-weather relations of to-day; that we should be as well prepared, and as well organized on land as Switzerland, a nation without a trace of militarism, and yet so thoroughly prepared and so thoroughly ready and able to defend herself that to-day her territory is inviolate, although she is surrounded by warring nations.

Belgium [conquered by Germany in 1914] to-day is an illustration of what may be expected from lack of adequate preparedness.

The great outstanding lesson of the war is that we must not trust to righteousness and fair dealing alone; we must be prepared to play our part, and while loving justice and dealing fairly with others, we must be always ready to do our full duty, and to defend our country with force if need be. If we do not, we shall always be helpless and at the mercy of our enemies. We can be strong, yet tolerant, just, yet prepared to defend ourselves against aggression.

U.S. Needs a Universal Military Service System

Another lesson is that our military establishment on land and sea should not be dependent upon a system of militia and volunteers. These will not be found adequate under the conditions of modern war, and above all we should appreciate the fact that our military system must be founded upon *equality of service, rich and poor alike*. We must while extending equality of privilege to all, including the thousands who are coming to us every day, insist upon equality of obligation by all. With the privileges of citizenship must go the obligations and responsibilities not only in peace but also in war.

We should take heed of the lessons of the past, and remember that the volunteer system has always failed us in our wars. Such experience as we have had in war in recent years has in no way prepared us for a war with a first-class nation prepared for war. We have never engaged in such a war unaided. This experience is one which is still before us. We should look upon service for the nation in the same way as we look upon the payment of taxes, or the compliance with the thousand and one laws and regulations which govern our everyday life.

We should take heed of the lessons of the past, and remember that the volunteer system has always failed us in our wars.

Relatively few people would voluntarily pay taxes even though they knew the money was to go to the best of purposes. They pay taxes because the law requires it. The people as a whole cannot be expected, nor can we with safety trust to their performing their military duties effectively, unless some general system of equal service for all who are physically fit, is prescribed, some system which will insure preparation in advance of war, some system which will *bear upon all alike*. The volunteer spirit is superb, but the volunteer system is not a dependable system to which to trust the life and security of the people, especially in these days when the highest degree of organization marks all nations with whom we may possibly have some day differences which will result in the use of force. The militia, willing as it is, cannot be depended upon as a reliable military asset. Its very method of control makes it an undependable force, and at times unavailable. The men and officers are not at fault; they have done all that could be expected under a system which renders efficiency almost impossible of attainment. The militia must be absolutely and completely transferred to Federal control; it must cease to be a State and become a Federal force, without any relationship whatever with the State.

The militia must have thoroughly trained reserves sufficient in number to bring it promptly to war strength. The infantry of the National Guard, as in the regular army, is maintained on a peace footing at rather less than half its maximum strength.

For a number of years we have been confronted by conditions which may involve the use of a considerable force of troops, a force exceeding the regular army and perhaps even the regular army in conjunction with the militia. This means that a thousand or more men would have to be added to each regular and National Guard infantry regiment to bring it to full strength. In the National Guard only a small proportion of the men have had long service and thorough training, and if brought to full strength through the injection of a thousand practically untrained men it would mean these regiments would go to the front with not over 30 per cent of well-trained men. In other words, they would be military assemblages of well-meaning, but undisciplined and untrained individuals, and unless we are to repeat the experiences of '98 [Spanish-American War] it will be necessary to hold them for several months in camp and put them through a course of the most intensive training. It is probable that if they are called it will be under an emergency which will not permit such training, and we shall see again the scenes of '98, untrained, willing boys, imperfectly equipped under inexperienced officers, rushed to the front, willing but a more or less useless sacrifice.

The Dangers of Military Weakness

Another great lesson should be to heed no longer those false prophets who have been proclaiming that the day of strife has passed, and that everything is to be settled by arbitration; prophets of the class who obstructed preparation in England [before the Great War], who decried universal military training, and all but delivered her into the hands of her enemies.

2

Preparedness Undermines American Democracy and Liberty

Oswald Garrison Villard

Oswald Garrison Villard (1872–1949), a lifelong pacifist and antimilitarist, hailed from a notable family of social reformers that included his renowned grandfather, antislavery agitator William Lloyd Garrison. Following in his father's footsteps, Villard became publisher and editor of the New York *Evening Post*. By World War I, he had become the editor of the *Nation*, which he helped make an influential voice for liberal reform and peace. In this 1916 essay, Villard assails American military-preparedness advocates and the military establishment. He believed that the vital American principle of civilian control of the military was being undermined by the military elite in the United States. According to Villard, fundamental American freedoms, like freedom of speech, were endangered by the pro-preparedness legislation and the growing power of the military. However, Villard remained hopeful that the American people would accept the appeal to reason and peace and would resist the growing militarism. His arguments reveal the deep American strain of pacifism, antimilitarism, and anti-imperialism that shaped the thinking of opponents of war in the World War I era.

The significance of preparedness, we are told, lies merely in the fact that Americans believe that our experiment in democracy is the most precious thing on earth; that it is

Oswald Garrison Villard, "Preparedness in Militarism," *Annals of the American Academy of Political and Social Science*, July 1916.

of greater moment to all the world than any other experiment in human government, and that, for it, Americans are as ready and as willing to die as were their fathers in 1860 [Civil War] and their forefathers in the Revolution.

"Life," remarked to me the other day one who sits in the seats of the mighty, "is but a beautiful adventure, to be flung away for an ideal whenever the hour calls." So we must be ready to count no cost should the enemy [Germany] be at the door, particularly if that enemy should be one who typifies the greatest military efficiency the world has ever seen, who believes its experiment in monarchical socialism of far greater value to humanity than our own brand of democracy, but combines within itself a military autocracy we hold to be the greatest menace to mankind in modern times.

Dangers of a Military Buildup in America

And so we are counseled to take from our possible enemy the very things that have made him efficient and dangerous and become efficient and dangerous ourselves.

Not that we shall ever make war—*pace* [with all due respect to] 1846 [U.S.-Mexican War] and 1898 [Spanish-American War]—on anybody; merely that we shall follow in the footsteps of those who believe that the earth is ruled by fear, and that there is no other way to preserve peace than by being so armed that no one shall venture to attack us. And so we have gone about getting a "preparedness" which we are strenuously but falsely pretending will be ours when the legislation now before Congress passes, and so protect us at the close of the war in Europe, and even safeguard us should the present difficulties with Germany result in hostilities. As a matter of fact, the Army reorganization proposed will not be consummated for five years, nor the naval program until 1925 or 1927, by which time the present war will be fading into the background. . . .

Now, the real significance of this is that we have all at once, in the midst of a terrifying cataclysm, abjured [renounced] our faith in many things American. We no longer believe, as for 140 years, in the moral power of an America unarmed and unafraid; we believe suddenly that the influence of the United States is to be measured only by the number of our soldiery and our dreadnoughts [battleships]—our whole history to the contrary notwithstanding. The ardent efforts of both sides in the present European struggle at the outbreak of the war to win for their cause the enormous prestige of the sympathy and moral support of the United States—although "unprepared"—we overlook as if it were not the most outstanding fact of the year from Aug. 1, 1914, to Aug. 1, 1915.

A cardinal principle of our polity has always been the subordination of the military to the civil authority.

We are to deprive the world of the one great beacon light of a nation unarmed and unafraid, free from the admitted evils of militarism. We are to complete the vicious military circle of the world so that, if we do not desist, if the oppressed of the nations do not rise in revolt against the whole accursed military system, the United States will be doing more than any other nation to intensify the race between peoples as to which will be armed most and at the greatest cost, and it will be one of the most hated and dreaded. As [former British prime minister] Lord Rosebery has said, nothing since the beginning of the war has been as discouraging, for in Mr. [Woodrow] Wilson's advocacy of our new [military] policy there has not been up to this hour one single phrase to the effect that the United States will be ready and eager to lead the way to disarmament at the close of the war, and our five-year naval program, as its terms signify, is a program for preparedness years hence.

Civilian Control of the Military Now Threatened

Next, the preparedness policy signifies an entire change in our attitude toward the military as to whom we inherited from our forefathers suspicion and distrust. A cardinal principle of our polity has always been the subordination of the military to the civil authority as a necessary safeguard for the republic, particularly in our national councils, and as to all matters affecting national policy. Today, in our sudden worship of the expert in uniform, we are told that what we need is a national council of defense comprising, as one rear admiral suggests and some of our new-born leagues of safety advise, fifteen military and naval officers with only seven civilians graciously given places at the council board.

These men, it appears, sitting in secret session and responsible only to themselves, are to formulate the policies of the nation, congressmen to have no other function than to vote the necessary money, ships, and men, it not being theirs to reason why. In other words, the council is to be our Great General Staff, and, like its German prototype, it is to make our Congress vote first like the Reichstag [Germany's legislature] and ask questions afterwards—the questions to be answered only if the council deems it wise. Its members are not to be elected but are to be designated by act of Congress, once for all.

Already it is openly stated in the press that the power of the secretary of the Navy is to be curtailed by the present Congress, so that he shall not be able to overrule the naval men, thus putting the military directly above the civil. For this purpose the undeserved unpopularity of the present secretary of the Navy [Josephus Daniels] is being cleverly exploited, while the public is kept in ignorance of the fact that England, the greatest and most efficient naval power on earth, has never, not even in its direst hour, yielded to the navalists, but has kept the control of the fleets in the hands of its civilian Lords of the Admiralty. Simultaneously we hear demands that only our future admirals and generals, and no civilians, shall be permitted to be our secretaries of the Navy and of war.

The truth is that there are no experts the world over so utterly discredited as the military ones.

But our sudden worship of the military does not end here. In New York the legislature has just established military drill in all the boys' schools, while all boys between the ages of fifteen and nineteen not at work are to go to camp as soldiers in the summer. There was no public demand for this bill, but the militia wished it, and through it went. Not even in Germany has such a step been advocated, for there, in the home of militarism, gymnastic exercises have been recognized as better preparation for life and military service than military drill. It goes without saying that the smattering of military knowledge the boys will acquire will be of the slightest value, since it is not planned to let them live in trenches, handle bombs, or distribute liquid fire and poisonous gases, and the instruction is bound to be highly superficial.

Militarism Poses Danger to Free Speech

The bill was not debated and is in its form a model of how not to legislate. It strikes deliberately at one of the most sacred American liberties—the right of freedom of thought, of action, and of conscience—since it excepts not even Quakers [pacifist religious sect], as even England excepts them today. It goes without saying that, we of New York, owe this favor entirely to the German General Staff. Yet are we told that militarism has and can have no foothold among us! As a matter of fact, we are assured not only that the soldier and the sailor are as infallible as the pope at Rome but similarly beyond criticism. . . .

There is a deep significance in the demand by the *New York Times*, now one of the most ultra-conservative class organs in the world, that protestants [protesters] against preparedness should not be allowed to speak in public after the President made his first public utterance for preparedness. It is of the utmost significance as also showing that, as in Europe, free speech is in danger when it comes to the criticizing of the military class and its program. So the *Seven Seas*, the organ of the Navy League, has recently demanded that [North Carolina] Congressman [Claude] Kitchin be not allowed to speak on the floor of the House because of his opposition to a vast navy, which navy, a contributor to this same journal says, shall have no higher aim than to seize for us the lands of weaker peoples wherever they may be found.

Already some of our Tory [right-wing] newspapers have begun to admit that there is a military party in this country—a military party suddenly raised up to add one more to the innumerable problems of race, of labor, of capital, of church, and all the rest with which the country is afflicted. If further proof were needed that we are well along the road toward militarism, it surely lies in the recent demand for the dismissal of the assistant secretary of labor because he thinks soldiers a feudal anachronism [outmoded, obsolete]. Further instances could be multiplied; it is only necessary to recall the fierce outburst of indignation at the labor leader who dared to say that the working people in this country were not sufficiently well-governed to make them care to fight for their government and their country.

Now, if our military and naval experts were the shining lights they pretend to be, why is it that by their own admissions they have made ducks and drakes of their own Army and Navy? The maladministration of our submarines cannot, for instance, be laid at the doors of the civilian control of the Navy Department or those of Congress; nor can the inefficiency of our regiments be attributed to the fact that the secretary of war is not a military man. . . .

Military Men Have Repeatedly Blundered in the War

The truth is that there are no experts the world over so utterly discredited as the military ones. It was the all-wise German General Staff that urged the greatest political blunder of modern times, the invasion of Belgium, as it was the German Navy Staff which ordered the sinking of the *Lusitania* and thereby horrified the world by this unparalleled act of barbarism. The generals who began this war to the world—where are most of them? Where are the Austrian and Russian generalissimos? [French general Joseph] Joffre survives as yet, and so does [German general Paul] Von Hindenburg. [General and Minister of War Horatio] Kitchener hangs by a thread. [British general] Sir John French, like many another, is in retirement, while the frightful slaughter at the Dardanelles, like that at Verdun, spells the shattering of many another reputation that deemed itself wise enough to lay down the law to civilians. The German General Staff—what has become of its certainty that it could take Paris in a month, that the raw levies [troops] of Kitchener would not fight, that Zeppelin [airship] raids over London would terrify the hearts of brave Englishmen? And what soldier truly foresaw trench warfare or the rise of the submarine or the invincibility of coast defenses?

Yet in this very hour, when the military the world over ought to be in the dust, we Americans are told that we must as blindly accept their decrees as did the poor, deluded German people in the years leading up to its present catastrophe. Critics are warned, moreover, not to point out that every military or naval officer is a biased expert, since he never fails to urge more men and more ships to his own personal profit, for this is already beginning to smack of high treason. We are, of course, wholly certain that we can never be quite like the Germans; therefore, a military caste is quite unthinkable among us—and yet we have the word of the secretary of the Navy that one high officer has told him that the only persons who are properly equipped to judge of the needs and conditions of the Navy are officers whose fathers and grandfathers served in our fleet before them! Who is there who has come into contact with our Navy life on its family and social side who has not been struck by its tendencies to snobbishness and aristocracy?

The air has been full of charges during the passage of the Army Bill by the Senate of the existence of two lobbies, that of the National Guard and that of those favoring a Continental Army. Both sides seem to the outsider to have proved their charges as to the existence of those lobbies, in addition to the existence of the regular army one, which a Cabinet officer once described to me as "the ablest, the most dangerous, and the most successful" lobby that ever came to Washington. We are creating in the National Guard a political machine of such power that already regular Army officers are asking whether Congress has not created a Frankenstein to destroy them. . . .

What it all means is that we are putting the emphasis upon the wrong things in life, on the old *de*structive military policy that holds out no hope for a better world, instead of on the *con*structive policy of facing squarely toward a world federation, or at least the freeing of the world from the old fear of one nation by another, a world whose militarism is the most successful device yet invented by tyrants, like the czar of Russia, for keeping their subjects despotically enslaved. It is a militarism which eats up such vast treasures in wood and iron and steel as to make ridiculous even in our unprepared country any campaign for the preservation of national resources. What will that avail if our defense bill next year is to be more than half a billion of dollars?

An Appeal for Reason and Peace Preparedness

Surely so intelligent a people as our own is not long thus to be deceived as to the significance of the new use of the old enslaving cries of patriotism, of national safety, of rallying about the flag. . . . For us, too, the paths of military glory "lead but to the grave"—to the despair that wrings the hearts of Europe and of England for all who stop to think of the losses to the world from a war which could never have come but for the armies and navies built up for defensive purposes and the war parties born of them, the real reason for which war no man knoweth. American sanity and intelligence will speedily see that the outcry from more soldiers and ships comes not from the masses of the people, but from the fortunate classes in life, and particularly from the very classes that have heretofore battened upon every special privilege. The coming of "preparedness" spells but a new phase of the old battle of democracy against privilege.

The coming of "preparedness" spells but a new phase of the old battle of democracy against privilege.

American sanity and intelligence and wisdom ought to see to it, when the war excitement is over and news of preparedness is no longer featured in the press . . . that their government face the other way. Indeed, for right-thinking people this is the time to let the time-serving and compromising [Wilson] administration in Washington know that they expect of it the highest "preparedness" in the form of a readiness to take the lead at the peace conference in proposing international disarmament or in calling a conference for this purpose simultaneously with the peace conference. As Mr. [Robert] Lansing [secretary of state] and Mr. Wilson rise to this opportunity, so will their final standing be at the bar of history.

It is idle to say that there are international problems beyond solution; that there is no way out of the present low estate of the world; that its animal passions cannot be checked. Behold in Paris there are now sitting the representatives of eight nations who are legislating not merely as to measures for carrying on the war against the Central Powers but as to such questions as a joint-tariff system, low telephone and telegraph tolls, an international statute as to the licensing of corporations, as to bankruptcies, yes, even as to the losses resulting from the theft of bonds, and as to the false designation of merchandise.

Now, if these great nations can take time and thought in the middle of a war they believe to be one of life and death to legislate together as to these things, who shall say that after this frightful bloodshed they cannot be led by the great

American republic to legislate on other far more vital themes? He who doubts belongs in the class with those who despair of humanity; who see nothing to be gained by tackling world-old evils because they are old; who bow down before brute passion and would touch neither the social evil, nor any social evil, nor smallpox, nor cancer, nor crime, nor ignorance, nor poverty, because of their age.

Against the god of might; against the god of force; against the policy of murder of millions by millions, there will be American citizens to protest as long as there are stars in their courses. Against every preparation for war men henceforth will rise to say *no*, even with their backs to the wall and rifles in front of them. For there is no slavery in the world like this to arms, none that today so checks the growth of liberty, of democracy, of the coming of the kingdom of heaven on earth. They will bear readily and willingly imputations of fanciful, unpractical idealism, of lack of patriotism; only it must never be said of them that they were unfaithful to their faith or that they were ever at peace with militarism, or that they were afraid to die for their ideals, or that they were traitors to the Prince of Peace [Jesus Christ] in thought or deed.

3

America Must Adopt Universal Military Service

Anne Rogers Minor

Anne Rogers Minor was a Connecticut artist and a leader in the patriotic organization the Daughters of the American Revolution in the World War I and postwar era. In this excerpt from a speech she delivered in 1916, Minor condemns American military weakness at a time of destructive war in Europe. The United States, she believes, cannot rely on pacifist sentiment in the face of German aggression in Europe and a possible assault on the United States. Minor argues that while peace is the goal of American policies, peace is achievable only by countering foreign (especially German) military power with American military power. She believes the U.S. military should institute universal service, modeling itself after Switzerland's efficient citizen army, which requires the service of the entire male population.

The war in Europe, terrible and hateful as it all is, is awakening a new patriotism in the United States. We see clearly the weakness of our position when forced to make demands of other nations. We see our almost defenseless coasts, our slow-growing navy and our very inadequate army. The grim realization of these facts is forced upon us, and we now know it would be criminal for us to persist longer in our traditional policy of unpreparedness

Anne Rogers Minor, "Peace Through National Defense," *Scientific Monthly*, April 1916, pp. 385–89.

and ignorance—a policy which has continued from the beginnings of the republic and which cost us more in blood, treasure and needless war than anything else in our history.

The people of the United States want peace, and we look for some method of assuring ourselves not only of the continuance of the peace which we now enjoy, but more than that, for the acquisition of power to help promote peace in other nations. We want national defense not for war, but to promote more perfect peace. It was a soldier, William Tecumseh Sherman, who said: "The legitimate object of war is more perfect peace."

America Needs a Policy of Peace Through Strength

How are we to maintain that peace which we have long enjoyed, that peace which is the highest ideal of our national life and without which we can not preserve the free institutions which our forefathers fought to establish? How are we to help to promote peace in other nations without the strength to make our protests effective. The answer is national defense, or power to enforce peace. In other words, that power which inspires such respect for us in other nations as will forbid their attacking us. No truer words were ever spoken than these of [American writer] Bayard Taylor's "Peace the offspring is of Power."

If carried to extremes [pacifism] would amount to no less than treason in hours of national peril.

Up to a little more than a year ago we did not believe that such a war as is being waged in Europe to-day was possible. We had hoped that war between civilized nations was a thing of the past, but our hopes were suddenly blasted when the most enlightened nations of the earth were caught in the same passions of war as the veriest [utmost] savages, less indiscriminately cruel perhaps, but just as blind in their frenzy of patriotic love and hate. These events have proved only too clearly that, no matter how highly civilized nations may appear to be, when their national safety seems at stake, or their national interests menaced, civilization and restraint are thrown to the winds, treaties and compacts are forgotten, whole races spurred by sudden savage hatred plunge headlong into war to the death with other races whom they hailed a short time before as friends and brothers. In the light of these facts, it is folly to say that war and aggression are things of the past, and that national humility and confidence in our own good intent, and in the high moral civilization of our neighboring nations, are sufficient guards against attack and disaster. We must profit by the lessons from the battlefields of Europe and not allow the futile and emotional cries of theorists and reformers for "peace, peace when there is no peace" blind us to the stern facts and realities which confront us and threaten not only our peace but our national existence.

Dangers of Pacifism and Military Weakness

A no doubt well-intentioned, but misguided, movement is being agitated among us which threatens to sap the strength of the nation and if not arrested bids fair to rob us of many of the sturdy qualities which are the mainstay of the republic. I refer to pacificism [pacifism] or the theory of "peace at any price"—a doctrine of absolute non-resistance. We must remember that we should not exist as a nation to-day if the men of '76 [the American Revolution] had believed in this theory. If carried to extremes it would amount to no less than treason in hours of national peril. When ordinarily sensible and high-minded people say to me that, even if an invader should approach our shores, we should let him enter and take possession, that we should offer no resistance, but allow him to violate our sacred liberties, I am lost in bewilderment at the kind of mind or soul which seems so lost to the fundamental instincts of self-defense implanted in the whole animate creation. Are we to put our faith in peace ships [automaker and peace advocate Henry Ford sponsored a futile voyage of peace-seeking activists to Europe in 1915] while the doctrine of brute force, the self-acknowledged creed of one great nation [Germany] that "Might is Right" still stalks abroad in the world, leaving its trail of blood and death on the fair fields of Europe? Shall we put our faith in peace ships when the ships of militarism cross the ocean and train their engines of death on our defenseless shores? God forbid that any such sentimental folly should ever replace the spirit of America, the spirit that made us a nation, the spirit that actuated the men of Concord and Lexington and Valley Forge. To imagine such a possibility is an insult to the memory of those patriots who sprang to the defense of their home-land against tyranny and outrage; an insult to their brave wives and daughters and sweethearts who bade them go in God's name, and then did men's work at home that the nation might live. We see this spirit to-day in the women of France, yet there are those who dare to summon them to talk of peace in conventions, while their homes are burning and their land is devastated and their husbands and sons are slain by the ruthless god of "Might is Right." What they want now is not "peace at any price." They want the kind of peace that can never be broken again. Is pacificism likely to bring this about? Can pacificism stay the onward course of a triumphant militarism armed to the teeth? Could pacificism have helped Belgium [invaded and occupied by Germany in 1914] in her hour of horror and need? Is it a man's part, or a woman's either, for that matter, to stand by idly theorizing, while the strong attack the weak, end treaties are proclaimed to be naught but scraps of paper? [In 1914, German chancellor Theobald von Bethmann Hollweg dismissed an 1839 treaty guaranteeing Belgian neutrality as a "scrap of paper."] What constitutes the binding force of a treaty in the mind of a nation that can so regard a treaty? Obviously nothing but a gun, since agreements and promises mean nothing. Insidious and secret war is already being waged upon us, a neutral nation, within our own borders by conspirators and spies to whom treaties and honor mean nothing. Our peace is threatened, our right to pursue our industrial interests undisturbed has been violated; our right to travel the high seas is denied; and American lives are sacrificed; internal disorders and lawlessness are instigated by the same power that trampled defenseless Belgium under foot. What are we going to do about it? After nine months of silence we uttered a protest against the slaughter of our citizens at sea and the violation of every sentiment of humanity and civilization. "What are you going to do about it?" was the reply, as plainly said as though uttered in words, and then the Arabic [British passenger ship sunk in August, 1915; two Americans were killed] was sunk. We were told to keep off the high seas, where we have a right to go in pursuit of lawful business; we were told to keep from taking passage on ships of belligerents, even though they were innocent merchantmen, so that violations of international law and humanity might go on undisturbed. And pacificists would have us keep off, and continue the policy of polite letter-writing, while more innocent lives are sacrificed to the god of Might-is-Right. If we had had something besides ink to feed the power of Mr. Wilson's pen the results might have been different. But we had not and Germany knew it. "The pen is mightier than the sword" in all cases except— that of a scrap of paper. If human liberty, civilization and self-government go down to final death in the trenches of Europe under the assaults of [German] militarism, will a defenseless pacifism save us from a like fate?

Can pacifism stay the onward course of a triumphant militarism armed to the teeth?

Pacificists tells us they do not mean disarmament, but they do mean that we should not increase our present total inadequate defenses.

Disarmament would be a splendid thing under certain conditions; it is what we all want; but to be effective it must be universal and simultaneous. We believe that through national defense this dream of disarmament will eventually come true. It is not true now, and until mankind reaches a stage of development that will admit of complete disarmament, our only safety lies in increasing our defenses.

The Swiss Army Should Be Our Model

There is no equality between one man armed and another man disarmed, and so it is with nations. Stable and equal conditions of peace can exist only between equally armed nations or equally disarmed nations, such as the United States and Canada. But between armed Europe and an unarmed America there is no equality and therefore there can be no security of continued peace. In the midst of the raging "sea of war" in Europe to-day there is what has been well named a little "island of peace." This is the wonderful little nation of Switzerland, respected, untouched, inviolate. And why? Because she is a nation armed to the teeth—every citizen a trained soldier. She is equal to her armed neighbors, yet without standing army or militaristic methods. Opposed to militarism, on the one hand, as strongly as she is opposed to "peace at any price" doctrines, on the other, she nevertheless maintains herself in a condition of continued peace even in the midst of surrounding war. While we in America stand around theorizing, and talking of universal peace in conventions and sending out peace ships to ask the dogs of war in Europe please to let go of each other's throats, this little country has turned itself into a nation of soldiers through a system of voluntary compulsory military service—voluntary because the nation voluntarily chose to submit itself to this means of national defense. More thoroughly democratic than we are ourselves, they have nevertheless realized that compulsory universal service is their only guarantee of national independence, and they have had since 1874 a veritable citizen army, in which every able-bodied citizen is a trained soldier and not one, except the general and his staff, a professional military man. To an article in *The National Geographic Magazine* for November, 1915, I am indebted for these facts and for the following figures. With a smaller population than that of Massachusetts and an area twice the latter's size, Switzerland can mobilize 240,000 trained soldiers in twenty-four hours. At the same rate we could mobilize 8,000,000. Besides these men, the Swiss have as many more in reserve, so that under this system we could have in the field a trained army of 16,000,000 men within twenty-four hours. The founders of our country laid down the same idea of a citizen soldiery; the only difference is, the Swiss have put it into serious practise, while we theorize and make laws which we never enforce. In principle, every [American] citizen is supposed to join the militia. Does he? And how many Americans know how to shoot to hit the mark, or have ever handled a gun? As a sharp contrast, the Swiss boy begins at ten years of age to take the gymnastics that fit him for military training, and he learns how to shoot like William Tell—substituting bullets for arrows. Every man cheerfully sacrifices a definite amount of his time toward the maintenance of the one thing dear to every Swiss—as to every American—his independence as a citizen of a free country, and the amount of time is exceedingly little. During the first year of liability to military service at the age of seventeen, he gives up seventy-five days, but only eleven days in each successive year.

His training is in the field, not in drill rooms, and he spends less on military taxes than any other nation. The burdens of preparedness are thus spread over the whole nation, and lie heavy upon no one individual. There are no "crack" regiments; no picking and choosing in the service. Each man goes where he is sent and can serve best. There is no caste system. Brains and ability win the high places; all start from the ranks. Our militia system has much to learn before it can be compared with the Swiss citizen army of defenders—for defenders they are. Not one foot of territory do they wish to acquire. Not a blow would they strike in aggression, but let him who strikes at them beware what he does! This is the ideal of national defense, which is the inalienable right of every man, of every woman, of every nation to defend itself against attack. Herein lie self-respect and a national dignity impervious to insult, because it is above insult. "Though surrounded on all sides by belligerent millions" (to quote from the aforesaid article) whose interests might be served by asking her to step out of their path, Switzerland to-day stands an island of peace in a sea of war, because she has prepared to maintain her neutrality and her freedom, or at least to exact such a price for them that none of the nations at war can afford to pay for their violation." What an object lesson for us. While in a country so large as ours it would be the height of folly to give up our regular standing army—say rather, it should be increased—it ought to be practicable to so remodel our militia as to approach nearer to the wonderful efficiency of the citizen army of Switzerland. If to such an army we would but add an adequate navy and sea-coast defense, we should be invincible. This would not militarize us as a nation; it would train us simply in efficient self-defense, whereby alone we can inspire, respect and maintain peace and liberty.

4

Americans Must Act Against the Dangers of Militarism

Crystal Eastman

Crystal Eastman (1881–1928) was a labor lawyer, journalist, feminist, and radical peace advocate. Believing that war and militarization endangered American progress, Eastman opposed both American entry into World War I and the campaign for military preparedness. The following report by Eastman was published in the reform journal, the *Survey*, on behalf of her organization, the American Union Against Militarism. To halt the war, Eastman urged peace supporters to back President Woodrow Wilson's December 1916 initiative to obtain peace terms from the belligerent powers and have the United States help organize a peace conference. Eastman also strongly supported a congressional amendment proposed by antipreparedness representative Walter Hensley. The amendment was to slash navy spending on warships if President Wilson succeeded in arranging a postwar peace conference that undertook steps toward disarmament. Finally, Eastman's report attacks the rising clamor for universal military service that she believed benefited the capitalist status quo and threatened essential American freedoms.

The radical peace movement, barely two years old, which is America's best answer to the war in Europe, has three main emphases: to stop the war in Europe; to or-

Crystal Eastman, "War and Peace," *Survey*, December 30, 1916, pp. 363–64.

ganize the world for peace at the close of the war; and to guard democracy (or such beginnings of democracy as we have in America) against the subtle dangers of militarism.

The radical peace movement . . . is America's best answer to the war in Europe.

With regard to the first aim, the moment of achievement seems to be at hand. Surely the President's note [of December 18, 1916, asking all the warring powers to state their peace terms, and pledging a U.S. peace role] makes the possibility of neutral action for peace almost immediate. If now we can gather together and express an overwhelming public opinion in support of that note our task will be done. The liberal and pacifist groups in the belligerent countries will do the rest.

Hensley Bill to Encourage Peace and Disarmament

As for international federation [a league or association of nations] at the end of the war, this is the supreme moment for action. We have the hope of the world in those Hensley [after Congressman Walter Hensley of Missouri] clauses of the navy law which request the President to summon the nations into conference at the close of the war to "consider disarmament" and organize for peace. The establishment of an international tribunal to settle disputes between nations has become a political possibility. We, the United States of America, through the action of our Congress, have taken the first step.

To make the Hensley clauses live in the mind of every American, to make them dominate the thoughts of the President, to make them ring through Europe as a promise of relief [from war], to make them known throughout South America as a guarantee of our good faith, to accomplish this *now* before the war is over—and then at its close to create such a demand for action on them that President Wilson will not sleep until he has written and dispatched to the heads of all the governments a classic summons to the World Congress which shall end war! There is a New Year's resolution for every pacifist in America.

But what shall we do, meanwhile, about the growing demand for compulsory military training and service in this country?—a demand stimulated by the self-interest of capitalists, imperialists and war traders, but supported by the sincere emotions of thousands who call themselves democrats? To defeat this combination we need the constant, uncompromising opposition of all those lovers of liberty who can *think*. We must make this great American democracy know, as we know, that military training is bad for the bodies and minds and souls of boys; that free minds, and souls undrilled to obedience are vital to the life of democracy. We must make them see the difference between equality and freedom; if forced military service is "democratic," in the same sense prison life is democratic.

Forced military service is "democratic," in the same sense prison life is democratic.

To repeal conscription where it has crept into our laws, to keep Congress from passing the Chamberlain Bill [after Oregon senator George Chamberlain] for universal [military] training, to keep the other states from following New York [which had adopted a statewide military program]—to hold the fort for liberty over here, until the nations are actually gathering to establish organized lasting peace—until, in short, every fool can see the folly of war preparations—that is the pacifists' third task for 1917. It is a task worthy of the grimmest and the gayest fighters among us.

Chapter 3

The Decision for War

1

The United States Declared War in Response to the German Threat to American Prestige and Security

Ernest R. May

In the following excerpt, historian Ernest R. May traces some of the final steps that led the United States into war against imperial Germany in early 1917. May views President Woodrow Wilson as a reluctant warrior who still hoped in January 1917 for a negotiated settlement to avoid American intervention. May argues here that hawkish German leaders forced Wilson to move toward war by launching an all-out submarine offensive against both neutral (U.S.) and belligerent shipping beginning on February 1, 1917. Germany's radical military escalation threatened U.S. prestige as a major world power and, hence, its national security. Wilson needed to react forcefully on behalf of American principles and interests, May argues. With his peaceful options seemingly exhausted, Wilson chose war. Ernest May is a professor of American history at Harvard University. He is the author of *Strange Victory: Hitler's Conquest of France* and *Knowing One's Enemies: Intelligence Analysis Before the Two World Wars.*

Ernest R. May, *The World War and American Isolation, 1914–1917.* Cambridge, MA: Harvard University Press, 1966. Copyright © 1959 by the President and Fellows of Harvard College. All rights reserved. Reproduced by permission.

When Wilson learned of the new German submarine campaign [beginning February 1, 1917], he had no reason to believe that Germany had made a final choice between war and peace. Twice in 1915 and once in 1916 the German government had seemed to challenge the United States, only to back down before the President's patient firmness. The new announcement was more abrupt than the proclamations of 1915 and 1916—submarine operations were to begin immediately. It was also more thoroughgoing. But it could still be read as a mere test of America's toughness.

The President's immediate problem was to manifest his unyielding opposition to the U-boat. The obvious course was to break relations with Germany. Such had been the threat in the *Sussex* ultimatum,[1] and [presidential adviser Edward M.] House and [Secretary of State Robert] Lansing counseled Wilson against doing anything less. Both argued that America's prestige could not be maintained if the President merely sent a new note of protest. Lansing laid so much stress on this point that his words deserve quotation:

> I said that if we failed to act I did not think we could hold up our heads as a great nation and that our voice in the future would be treated with contempt by both the Allies and Germany. . . . I felt that the greatness of the part which a nation plays in the world depends largely upon its character and the high regard of other nations; that I felt that to permit Germany to do this abominable thing without firmly following out to the letter what he had proclaimed to the world we would do, would be to lose our character as a great power and the esteem of all nations; and that to be considered a "bluffer" was an impossible position for a nation which cherished self-respect.

The President did not at once accept his advisers' opinions. Lansing, who had already said that severance of relations would mean war, spoke as if a break would be a mere preliminary to hostilities, but Wilson did not entirely trust his Secretary of State, and he was not ready to accept war as a foregone conclusion.

1. April 1916 U.S. warning to Germany to cease submarine attacks or face a break of diplomatic relations; *Sussex* was an unarmed French steamer sunk with several U.S. casualties.

He did decide that he had to break relations. Nothing less seemed apt to make an impression in Berlin. If a note were sent instead, it would have to contain an ultimatum even stronger than that implicit in the *Sussex* note, and a threat might be more risky than a mere break in relations. Wilson discussed with House the possibility of deferring the break until an actual sinking occurred, but the colonel strongly advised prompt action. "If we waited for the overt act," House noted in his diary, "they would believe we had accepted their ultimatum. I had in mind, too, the effect it would have on the Allies. We would not be nearly so advantageously situated if we waited, as if we acted promptly." The President reluctantly agreed and deferred the break only until he could give prior notice to Senator [William J.] Stone. On February 3 he went before Congress to announce the severance of relations.

The Germans seemed to be behaving, [Wilson] commented, like madmen.

Through most of February, 1917, Wilson held to his policy of patient firmness. He did not underrate the force of the new challenge. The Germans seemed to be behaving, he commented, like madmen. Nor did he exaggerate his chances. When House and Lansing foretold failure, he did not dispute. So long as the faintest hope remained, however, he had to continue his earlier policy.

He made every effort to convince the Germans of his resoluteness. When giving public notice of the break in relations, he used menacing language. "[I]f American ships and American lives should in fact be sacrificed . . .," he declared, "I shall take the liberty of coming again before the Congress, to ask that authority be given me to use any means that may be necessary for the protection of our seamen and our people." Of America's principles he asserted, "These are the bases of peace, not war. God grant we may not be challenged to defend them." When the suggestion reached him through neutral channels that the United States and Germany negotiate while the submarine campaign continued, he refused point-blank. The precondition of any resumption of relations, he let it be known, was a return to the *Sussex* pledge [Germany's May 1916 conditional promise to avoid sinking unresisting merchant shipping without warning] of the preceding spring.

He insisted, at the same time, on remaining as patient as ever. Lansing favored proclaiming Germany an international outlaw. Various members of the cabinet urged the defensive arming of American merchant vessels. But Wilson declined all such advice. Although he recognized the need for military precautions, he warned the Secretary of War to give "no basis . . . for opinion abroad that we are mobilizing." So long as there remained any chance of diplomatic success, he risked no provocative move.

He did use every kind of diplomatic pressure. Inviting other neutrals to join in breaking relations, he sought to show Germany how world opinion disapproved of her act. He also hoped undoubtedly that she would see the immensity of the dangers that she ran. [State Department official Frank L.] Polk conferred with the Swiss minister, and House talked with the representative of the Netherlands. Although Wilson had told Congress that he took it for granted other neutrals would join him, China was the only one to do so. The Swiss government begged off on the ground of its vulnerable situation. The Dutch minister commented that European neutrals had been trying for two years to obtain Wilson's cooperation. Since he had not helped them, they were not prepared to rescue him. The President's effort to show the Germans that they were alienating all neutrals was unsuccessful.

He could seek to impress them with the danger of alienating the United States alone. House, who understood Wilson's purposes, used every channel to convey "some idea of the potential force of this country from a military, financial, and industrial viewpoint." Wilson meanwhile allowed the Germans to be warned gently of the loss to be suffered if Belgian relief stopped. What he wanted to do, of course, was not to provoke the Germans but to bring them to a realization of the stakes with which they were gambling.

A Bid to Divide the German-Led Central Powers

He sought also to bring pressure of another kind upon Germany. Reports from the American embassy in Vienna had given a picture of near despair. Although Austria joined her ally in proclaiming unrestricted submarine warfare, [Austro-

Hungarian foreign minister] Count [Ottakar] Czernin appealed to the United States to continue her efforts for a peace with "no victors and no vanquished." The President elected not to break relations with Austria or with Bulgaria and Turkey. There existed a possibility of inducing Germany's allies to bring her to her senses or alternatively of frightening Germany with the prospect of a break-up in her own coalition.

The President sought, indeed, to pry the Central Powers apart. He directed Lansing to cable London, asking permission to offer Austria a separate peace with a promise that her territory would remain intact. Even though this scheme was at variance with principles which Wilson had already uttered, it held much promise. Austria might be emboldened to press for German conciliation of the United States. Or she might compel her ally to resume discussion of a general peace. In that case Wilson was prepared to offer Germany terms even more enticing than those outlined in the "peace without victory" message. "Four Bases of Peace," sketched by the President in early February, included equality of economic opportunity and naval disarmament. Another possibility was, of course, that Austria might actually be detached from America's prospective enemies. Since [British prime minister David] Lloyd George delayed his answer, no offer was made until after Wilson had lost nearly all hope of bringing the Germans to reason. The President asked Czernin to consider a separate peace and not to discuss it with Germany. At the outset, however, he must have considered the offer a tactic that might bring victory in the submarine controversy.

Among the conceivable devices by which the President could press or lure the Germans into concession, only one was not used. Wilson could have demonstrated his willingness to act against the Allies if only Germany would first abandon the U-boat. He had held out such a hope during earlier crises. Despite his own continuing anger at the blockade [of Germany] and the [British] blacklist [of American business firms trading with Germany], he did not do so in February, 1917. The only gesture in that direction was a curt note protesting a British decree that made part of the North Sea a defensive zone. In refraining from any other challenge to the Allies, Wilson may have been sidestepping criticism from Anglophiles whose support he would need if

Germany failed to give in. He may have held in mind the possibility that he might soon need cooperation from the Allied governments themselves. Or he may simply have recognized that having failed to press the Allies when U-boats were quiet he was not likely to impress the Germans with action at this stage. With this one exception, Wilson employed every pressure and enticement consistent with his basic policy. Although his chief effort failed when the European neutrals declined to join him, he was in no position to compel their cooperation. The quickness and adroitness of his tactics contrasted with his slowness and awkwardness in 1915. He had become a much more accomplished diplomatist. But his adversary was no longer the same. Diplomacy was of no avail against [hard-line German general Erich von] Ludendorff.

The Zimmermann Telegram and Deteriorating Relations with Germany

By the end of February [1917] Wilson had seen that patient firmness would no longer work. In earlier crises the German government had quickly shown a conciliatory disposition. Now there was no such sign. Swiss intermediaries reported Berlin willing to negotiate, it is true, but not to modify the U-boat campaign. Dispatches to the Department of State meanwhile told of frequent torpedoings. No American vessel happened to be sunk without warning, but submarine commanders were said to be ignoring neutral flags, and two Norwegian ships were among those destroyed. It appeared to be pure chance that no American citizens were among the dead. The occurrence of some critical incident was almost certain.

Three weeks after the break, moreover, Wilson received evidence that Germany anticipated war. The proof was [Foreign Secretary Arthur] Zimmermann's telegram to [German ambassador to Mexico Heinrich von] Eckhardt, proposing a German-Mexican-Japanese alliance in case of war. Intercepted by British naval intelligence more than a month before, its disclosure to [U.S. ambassador to Britain Walter Hines] Page had been delayed until the method could be concealed from the Germans. Page lost no time in cabling Wilson. The President thus had before him a document of unquestionable authenticity, indicating that Germany preferred war to abandonment of the U-boat campaign.

The Issue of Arming U.S. Merchant Ships

His principal advisers had already urged active measures of resistance. At the first cabinet discussion of breaking relations, several members had suggested arming American merchantmen. The President had agreed to let the State Department tell shipowners that they could arm, but he refused to supply guns and ammunition. [Secretary of the Treasury William G.] McAdoo and others became increasingly insistent that he change his decision. The Secretary of the Treasury argued that American vessels were staying in port out of fear. The result was not only injury to the American economy but indirect aid to Germany: the United States was in effect cooperating in the German blockade. At a cabinet meeting on February 23, McAdoo and those who sympathized with him became so demanding as to anger Wilson. He accused them of trying to push the country into war. One of the members referred to the session subsequently as "one of the most animated . . . that I suppose has ever been held under this or any other President."

Wilson Calls on Congress to Arm U.S. Ships

Not long after this meeting, Wilson decided partially to follow McAdoo's advice. He does not seem to have been so concerned as the Treasury Secretary over the timidity of American shippers. He believed that constitutionally he possessed the power to supply merchantmen with defensive armament. Yet he chose not to do so on his own authority. Instead he took the slower method of addressing Congress, asking for a gratuitous [unnecessary] grant of power and for a suitable appropriation. He delivered this request on February 26, three days after the turbulent cabinet session and two days after he learned of the Zimmermann note.

One obvious reason for addressing Congress instead of acting was, of course, to test sentiment. The election campaign of 1916 had displayed the firm hold of pacifism and neutralism on large segments of the public. Against Wilson's will and wishes, "He kept us out of war" had become the Democrats' most potent slogan. Toward the end of the campaign, the President commented to House, "I do not believe the American people would wish to go to war no matter how many Americans were lost at sea." He said much the same thing again early in 1917. Press summaries and comments by politicians indicated that a sharp change had occurred when Germany announced unrestricted warfare [on January 31, 1917]. The Senate's 78-5 approval of the severance of relations bore out this judgment. But Wilson undoubtedly remembered expert estimates proved wrong both by the Gore-McLemore resolutions [failed congressional resolutions banning Americans from traveling on belligerent vessels] and by the pacifist outbursts of the 1916 campaign. One good reason for asking Congress to authorize the arming of merchantmen was, as Wilson openly confessed, "to feel that the authority and the power of the Congress are behind me in whatever it may become necessary for me to do."

Wilson's Concern with Both U.S. and German Hawks

In addition to testing pacifist and neutralist strength, the appeal to Congress also served to frustrate the chauvinists [hawks]. Hardly had the Senate endorsed the break in relations before [Theodore] Roosevelt and his friends began to demand further steps. On February 23 the New York *Times* revealed that [Senator Henry Cabot] Lodge and other Republicans meant to block essential bills so that Wilson would have to call the new Congress into early session. Some members were reported complaisant [willing], feeling that the diplomatic situation made it desirable for the House to sit anyway. By obtaining the existing Congress' sanction not only to arm ships but also "to employ any other instrumentalities or methods that may be necessary . . . to protect our ships and our people," Wilson could counter the strongest arguments for a special session. He could hope thus to block jingo [hawkish] pressures from Congress.

Even so, it seems unlikely that Wilson was solely concerned with domestic opinion. His message to Congress was addressed to Germany as well as to America. Without actually taking a provocative step, he was making it clear that he would not permit Germany to win by default. At the same time, with passionate earnestness he asked the Germans to realize that he did not want war or even armed neutrality. In guarded language be even implied a possible willingness to negotiate the whole submarine issue afresh. He was not so much concerned with American commerce and travel, he asserted, as with "those great principles of compassion and of protection which mankind has sought to throw about human lives, the lives of noncombatants, the lives of men who are peacefully at work keeping the industrial processes of the world quick and vital, the lives of women and children and of those who supply the labour which ministers to their sustenance." His message to Congress of February 26, 1917, embodied the last adaptation of patient firmness. Intended to display the unity and resoluteness of America, it was meant as a final appeal to Germany to turn back.

As such it was a total failure. The House approved a resolution 403-13. The Senate indicated that it would have followed suit by something like 75-12. Although some neutralists approved of armed neutrality as a desperate substitute for war, these ballots reinforced the advice of [Press Secretary Joseph P.] Tumulty and others that the country would follow wherever the President led. A determined filibuster [long speeches to obstruct passage of Senate bills] by pacifists in the Senate prevented this sentiment from materializing as legislation. It also frustrated the President's hope of avoiding a special session. Most important of all, it denied him that clear demonstration of national unity which he hoped might bring the Germans to their senses. The importance which he attached to such a demonstration appeared in his angry comment upon the filibuster: "A little group of willful men, representing no opinion but their own, have *rendered the great Government of the United States helpless and contemptible.*"

Wilson's Reluctant Decision for War

On March 4 Wilson entered his second term. During part of early March he secluded himself in the White House, much as he had in the anguished interval after the sinking of the *Lusitania*. The policy contrived at that time had broken down. The President had to review once again the alternative of surrendering before the German challenge. The option earlier had been to risk war. The option now was war itself. Between March 7 and March 19 he wrestled with this choice. In the end he emerged, satisfied that the right and rational course was war.

Too little attention has been given to the address with which Wilson opened his second term. His biographers have passed it by. Yet it is the one document showing his state of mind on the eve of deciding for war, and its stresses are revealing. In it Wilson observed sadly that the United States had reached a point from which there was no turning back: "matters lying outside our own life as a nation and over which we had no control, . . . despite our wish to keep free of them, have drawn us more and more irresistibly into their own current and influence." The United States, he declared, had to be concerned with the peace that followed the war. The one hope of preserving a world in which America's peculiar values could thrive lay in a settlement that averted future wars, and such a peace could be achieved only if the United States exerted the influence to which her power and virtue entitled her. The President asserted, in other words, that a policy which sacrificed America's prestige and moral reputation would mortgage the welfare and happiness of generations yet to come.

In this same address Wilson laid heavy stress on the need for national unity. Some of it might be dismissed as rhetorical imitation, following the fashions of Jefferson and Lincoln. But its closing paragraphs cannot be read as mere flourishes [showiness]. Wilson pleaded with his hearers to understand:

> [I]t is imperative that we should stand together. We are being forged into a new unity amidst the fires that now blaze throughout the world. In their ardent heat we shall, in God's providence, let us hope, be purged of faction and division, purified of the errant humors of party and private interest, and shall stand forth in the days to come with a new dignity of national pride and spirit. . . . The thing I shall count upon, the thing without which neither counsel nor action will avail, is the unity of America—an America united in feeling, in purpose, in its vision of duty, of opportunity, and of service. . . . The shadows that now lie dark upon our path will soon be dispelled and we shall walk with the light all about us if we be but true to ourselves—to ourselves as we have wished to be known in the counsels of the world and in the thought of all those who love liberty and justice and the right exalted.

Defending American Prestige, Unifying Public Support

If Wilson spoke candidly as well as feelingly, then he entered his days in the wilderness sure of two things: first, that the prestige of the United States had to be maintained; second, that it was his duty as President to unify the people.

No one knows or can know what went through Wilson's mind in those decisive days of March. He talked revealingly to no one. Such letters as he wrote were formal or perfunctory [routine]. During much of the time his superb analytical powers undoubtedly sought every possible alternative. He had by this time acquired considerable knowledge and experience in international politics. Few emotional attachments remained to blur the precision of his thought. Over a period of more than two years he had canvassed the subject of German-American relations with a wide range of advisers, especially with his shrewd and perceptive friend, House. It is true that he could not foresee what actually was to happen in 1919 and after. Nor could he foretell Brest-Litovsk [a treaty dictated by Germany to Russia, enabling German troops to be shifted west to attack the Allies], the offensives of 1918, and the [American] expeditionary force of two million men. Otherwise, it can be assumed, he reviewed every consideration that any analyst has been able to imagine in restrospect.

The one clear alternative was that which Wilson had rejected before. He could surrender, asserting that American property losses would be the subjects of postwar claims. He could ask legislation in the spirit of the Gore and McLemore resolutions to prevent the loss of American life. There was no longer a compelling economic reason for resisting the German blockade. America had become so prosperous that she could afford to lose part of her trade with the Allies. The unrestricted submarine campaign had seemed thus far to be relatively ineffective. Statistics published at the beginning of March indicated only slight increases in Allied tonnage losses.

Nor was it evident that acquiescence would injure the visible security interests of the United States. Despite the Zimmermann note and other warnings of German activity in Latin America, Wilson had not retracted his earlier assertion to House that no European power offered an immediate menace to the United States. A relatively long period of recovery would be necessary for Germany, he had said, even if she triumphed in Europe. And he had little or no reason to suspect that Germany would win, even if the United States tolerated the U-boat blockade. Page warned him, it is true, that the Allies were on their last legs, but

Wilson had long made allowance for Page's excitable temper. Other reports from London, Paris, and even St. Petersburg exhaled confidence. No longer regarding the Allies as upholders of law and civilization, Wilson had said time and again that America's interest lay in a peace without victory. There was no reason for him to believe in March, 1917, that this interest precluded acquiescence in the recent German [unrestricted submarine warfare] decree.

What did make it impossible was the fact that it would sacrifice America's prestige and moral influence. At the outset of the submarine controversy it had seemed apparent that America would not live up to her potential if she allowed her citizens to be denied the free right of travel. Partly to demonstrate that the United States was a power entitled to respect and deserving of influence, Wilson had taken the cautious gamble of resisting indiscriminate U-boat warfare. Each subsequent diplomatic victory had committed America's prestige more deeply. The submarine issue had also become the symbol of Wilson's willingness to stand up for the rule of law, for international justice, and, as he termed it, for the rights of humanity. If he now retreated he would, in effect, prove America incapable of exercising influence compatible with her population, resources, and ideals. He would demonstrate her Pharisaism [hypocrisy], her inability to endure martyrdom for what she believed right. In view of his conviction that her own future turned upon her ability to prevent a recurrence of war, he simply could not accept the pacifist alternative.

Wilson's Reasons for Rejecting Armed Neutrality Option

Acquiescence was not, of course, the only alternative. Another was armed neutrality. American ships could be provided with guns. They could defend themselves against U-boats. The United States would thus be upholding her principles while waging only a very limited war. Professor Carlton J.H. Hayes of Columbia University had prepared a long and compelling memorandum outlining the virtues of this course. It would make clear that the United States opposed only Germany's illegal and immoral method of warfare. It would allow America to escape military involvement on the continent and leave her unentangled in the intricacies of Allied ambitions and European power rivalries. The

President had read this memorandum before asking Congress for power to arm merchantmen. From his address at that time and from other comments, it is evident that this alternative had some attraction for him. While it is comparatively simple to infer his reasons for rejecting pacifism, it is rather harder to sense the rationale that led him away from limited belligerency.

One consideration undoubtedly was the practical difficulty of devising a suitable policy. The Navy Department sketched for him the alternative methods of carrying out an armed neutrality. One was for American ships to acknowledge the legal right of U-boats to conduct visit and search but to resist unlawful attacks. A second was for them to treat German submarines as hostile craft when encountered inside the war zone. A third was to treat U-boats as hostile craft wherever met and to attack them on sight. Each course presented obvious difficulties. One invited torpedoings; the second risked them; the third was not very different from a state of war.

Armed neutrality in any form involved a further danger of blurring the issues. American merchantmen might err in sinking submarines. Especially if the United States were to follow the third of the navy's three forms of armed neutrality, American captains were likely to act in excess of zeal. The result might easily be an American *Baralong* [in August 1915 a British decoy ship, *Baralong*, used an American flag to surprise and sink a German U-Boat, inflaming German opinion] case, which the Germans might employ as a moral pretext for war. Armed neutrality would, in any case, allow Germany to choose her own time and occasion for opening hostilities.

U.S.-Germany Mistrust Reaches Critical Mass

Even so, Wilson could still have elected the alternative. He had always shown a disposition to postpone crises. It would not have been out of character for him to adopt a policy that threw the choice of peace or war back upon Berlin. The keys to his final decision probably lay first of all in his complete mistrust of Germany, secondly in his emphatic desire to preserve domestic unity, and thirdly in his conception of America's probable war effort.

He could no longer expect Germany to be deterred from any action by fear of war with the United States. Responses to the [U.S.] pressures applied during early February had indicated total indifference. Not only had Zimmermann asserted that there was no turning back, but a semiofficial newspaper (the Berlin *Lokal-Anzeiger*), quoted in the United States, had declared, "As to the neutrals—we can no longer be bothered by their opinions." In his message to Congress asking authority to arm ships, Wilson had referred to uncompromising statements by German officials and by the German press. The Zimmermann telegram itself had indicated no more than that Germany anticipated war. Wilson was more shocked apparently by the method of its dispatch. Zimmermann had sent the message to [German ambassador to the U.S. J.H. von] Bernstorff for forwarding, using State Department cable lines which had been opened for the sake of peace discussions. Coupled with Zimmermann's insouciant [carefree] admission that the telegram was genuine, this revelation seemed to demonstrate that Germany no longer saw any advantage in keeping the peace. The *coup de grâce* [finishing stroke, death blow] for any lingering hope came in [German chancellor or prime minister] Bethmann Hollweg's address to the Reichstag, delivered on the day after Wilson requested, power to arm merchantmen. According to the State Department's report of this speech, Bethmann spoke of America's "subjection to English power and control"; he declared that the severance of relations was meant neither to protect freedom of the seas nor to promote peace but only to help "starve Germany and increase bloodshed"; he ended by asserting, "now that our sincere desire to promote peace has met with nothing but ridicule at hands of our enemies there is no longer any retreat for us—nothing but 'Forward.'" It appeared from Wilson's perspective as if there were no longer a moderate party in Berlin. Whether the United States declared war or simply proclaimed an armed neutrality, Germany was likely in either case to treat her as an all-out enemy.

2

A War to Make the World Safe for Democracy

Woodrow Wilson

President Woodrow Wilson's war message of April 2, 1917, stands out as one of the most significant speeches in American history. Before a tense special session of Congress and an audience of nearly all the highest U.S. government officials, Wilson delivered an eloquent call to arms, infused with a sincere, even tragic sense of the high stakes of the moment. Whereas his leading political rival of the day, Theodore Roosevelt, had been eager for U.S. military participation in the conflict early on, Wilson had agonized and resisted mounting pressure for intervention until mid-March 1917. In his address, Wilson first states the reason for war: Germany's renewal of unrestrained submarine warfare since February 1917. This assault, he notes, has targeted neutral as well as belligerent shipping and resulted in a mounting loss of life. For Wilson this is, in effect, a German attack on the United States, which the nation must answer with a congressional declaration of war. Even more significant in Wilson's speech, however, is his definition of Germany as an autocratic regime menacing all Western democracies. Wilson then unveils his vision of a new world political order that must be the common policy of all of Germany's foes. He argues that America's primary war aims should be a world made secure for democracy, freedom of the seas, national self-determination, and a postwar league of democratic nations.

Woodrow Wilson, address to the United States Congress, Washington, DC, April 2, 1917.

I have called the Congress into extraordinary session because there are serious, very serious, choices of policy to be made, and made immediately, which it was neither right nor constitutionally permissible that I should assume the responsibility of making.

Germany Created Crisis by Abandoning Restraints on U-Boats

On the 3rd of February [1917], I officially laid before you the extraordinary announcement of the Imperial German government that on and after the 1st day of February it was its purpose to put aside all restraints of law or of humanity and use its submarines to sink every vessel that sought to approach either the ports of Great Britain and Ireland or the western coasts of Europe or any of the ports controlled by the enemies of Germany within the Mediterranean [Sea].

That had seemed to be the object of the German submarine warfare earlier in the war, but since April of last year the Imperial government had somewhat restrained the commanders of its undersea craft in conformity with its promise then given to us that passenger boats should not be sunk and that due warning would be given to all other vessels which its submarines might seek to destroy, when no resistance was offered or escape attempted, and care taken that their crews were given at least a fair chance to save their lives in their open boats. The precautions taken were meager and haphazard enough, as was proved in distressing instance after instance in the progress of the cruel and unmanly business, but a certain degree of restraint was observed.

The new policy has swept every restriction aside. Vessels of every kind, whatever their flag, their character, their cargo, their destination, their errand, have been ruthlessly sent to the bottom without warning and without thought of help or mercy for those on board, the vessels of friendly neutrals along with those of belligerents. Even hospital ships and ships carrying relief [supplies] to the sorely bereaved and stricken people of Belgium, though the latter were provided with safe conduct through the proscribed areas by the German government itself and were distinguished by unmistakable marks of identity, have been sunk with the same reckless lack of compassion or of principle.

I was for a little while unable to believe that such things would in fact be done by any government that had hitherto subscribed to the humane practices of civilized nations. International law had its origin in the attempt to set up some law which would be respected and observed upon the seas, where no nation had right of dominion and where lay the free highways of the world. By painful stage after stage has that law been built up, with meager enough results, indeed, after all was accomplished that could be accomplished, but always with a clear view, at least, of what the heart and conscience of mankind demanded.

This minimum of right the German government has swept aside under the plea of retaliation and necessity and because it had no weapons which it could use at sea except these which it is impossible to employ as it is employing them without throwing to the winds all scruples of humanity or of respect for the understandings that were supposed to underlie the intercourse of the world. I am not now thinking of the loss of property involved, immense and serious as that is, but only of the wanton and wholesale destruction of the lives of noncombatants, men, women, and children, engaged in pursuits which have always, even in the darkest periods of modern history, been deemed innocent and legitimate. Property can be paid for; the lives of peaceful and innocent people cannot be.

The present German submarine warfare against commerce is a warfare against mankind. It is a war against all nations. American ships have been sunk, American lives taken in ways which it has stirred us very deeply to learn of; but the ships and people of other neutral and friendly nations have been sunk and overwhelmed in the waters in the same way. There has been no discrimination. The challenge is to all mankind.

Each nation must decide for itself how it will meet it. The choice we make for ourselves must be made with a moderation of counsel and a temperateness of judgment befitting our character and our motives as a nation. We must put excited feeling away. Our motive will not be revenge or the victorious assertion of the physical might of the nation, but only the vindication of right, of human right, of which we are only a single champion. . . .

With a profound sense of the solemn and even tragical character of the step I am taking and of the grave responsibilities which it involves, but in unhesitating obedience to what I deem my constitutional duty, I advise that the Congress declare the recent course of the Imperial German government to be in fact nothing less than war against the government and people of the United States; that it formally accept the status of belligerent which has thus been thrust upon it; and that it take immediate steps, not only to put the country in a more thorough state of defense but also to exert all its power and employ all its resources to bring the government of the German Empire to terms and end the war. . . .

Neutrality Impossible When Autocratic Regimes Are Threats

Our object . . . is to vindicate the principles of peace and justice in the life of the world as against selfish and autocratic power and to set up among the really free and self-governed peoples of the world such a concert of purpose and of action as will henceforth ensure the observance of those principles. Neutrality is no longer feasible or desirable where the peace of the world is involved and the freedom of its peoples, and the menace to that peace and freedom lies in the existence of autocratic governments backed by organized force which is controlled wholly by their will, not by the will of their people. We have seen the last of neutrality in such circumstances. We are at the beginning of an age in which it will be insisted that the same standards of conduct and of responsibility for wrong done shall be observed among nations and their governments that are observed among the individual citizens of civilized states.

We have no quarrel with the German people. We have no feeling toward them but one of sympathy and friendship. It was not upon their impulse that their government acted in entering this war. It was not with their previous knowledge or approval. It was a war determined upon as wars used to be determined upon in the old, unhappy days when peoples were nowhere consulted by their rulers and wars were provoked and waged in the interest of dynasties or of little groups of ambitious men who were accustomed to use their fellowmen as pawns and tools. . . .

We are accepting this challenge of hostile purpose because we know that in such a government, following such methods, we can never have a friend; and that in the presence of its organized power, always lying in wait to accomplish we know not what purpose, there can be no assured security for the democratic governments of the world. We are now about to accept gage of battle with this natural foe to liberty and shall, if necessary, spend the whole force of the nation to check and nullify its pretensions and its power. We are glad, now that we see the facts with no veil of false pretense about them, to fight thus for the ultimate peace of the world and for the liberation of its peoples, the German peoples included: for the rights of nations great and small and the privilege of men everywhere to choose their way of life and of obedience.

U.S. Aim: A World Safe for Democracy

The world must be made safe for democracy. Its peace must be planted upon the tested foundations of political liberty. We have no selfish ends to serve. We desire no conquest, no dominion. We seek no indemnities for ourselves, no material compensation for the sacrifices we shall freely make. We are but one of the champions of the rights of mankind. We shall be satisfied when those rights have been made as secure as the faith and the freedom of nations can make them. . . .

It is a distressing and oppressive duty, gentlemen of the Congress, which I have performed in thus addressing you. There are, it may be, many months of fiery trial and sacrifice ahead of us. It is a fearful thing to lead this great peaceful people into war, into the most terrible and disastrous of all wars, civilization itself seeming to be in the balance. But the right is more precious than peace, and we shall fight for the things which we have always carried nearest our hearts—for democracy, for the right of those who submit to authority to have a voice in their own governments, for the rights and liberties of small nations, for a universal dominion of right by such a concert of free peoples as shall bring peace and safety to all nations and make the world itself at last free.

To such a task we can dedicate our lives and our fortunes, everything that we are and everything that we have, with the pride of those who know that the day has come when America is privileged to spend her blood and her might for the principles that gave her birth and happiness and the peace which she has treasured. God helping her, she can do no other.

3

The War Will Benefit American Big Business, Not the People

George W. Norris

George W. Norris (1861–1944) was a progressive Republican senator from Nebraska who resisted the nation's drift toward war after 1914. In the following excerpt from his April 4, 1917, Senate speech explaining his vote against the declaration of war, Norris argues that Wall Street financial interests are the driving force behind the decision for war. Investors who have made large loans to the Allies seek military intervention to assure repayment. Munitions manufacturers who make large profits from selling armaments also support the war. Likewise, many large newspaper and news service companies influence public opinion with prowar propaganda. Norris believes that the human and financial burdens of war fall on the ordinary American, while only the wealthy and powerful profit handsomely from war.

W hile I am most emphatically and sincerely opposed to taking any step that will force our country into the useless and senseless war now being waged in Europe, yet, if this [war] resolution passes, I shall not permit my feeling of opposition to its passage to interfere in any way with my duty either as a senator or as a citizen in bringing success and victory to American arms. I am bitterly opposed to my country entering the war, but if, notwithstanding my oppo-

George W. Norris, address to the United States Senate, Washington, DC, April 4, 1917.

sition, we do enter it, all of my energy and all of my power will be behind our flag in carrying it on to victory.

The resolution now before the Senate is a declaration of war. Before taking this momentous step, and while standing on the brink of this terrible vortex, we ought to pause and calmly and judiciously consider the terrible consequences of the step we are about to take. We ought to consider likewise the route we have recently traveled and ascertain whether we have reached our present position in a way that is compatible with the neutral position which we claimed to occupy at the beginning and through the various stages of this unholy and unrighteous war.

U.S. Policy Has Been Partial to Britain

No close student of recent history will deny that both Great Britain and Germany have, on numerous occasions since the beginning of the war, flagrantly violated in the most serious manner the rights of neutral vessels and neutral nations under existing international law, as recognized up to the beginning of this war by the civilized world.

We could have said . . . American ships and American citizens will go into these [British and German war] zones at their own . . . risk.

The reason given by the President [Woodrow Wilson] in asking Congress to declare war against Germany is that the German government has declared certain war zones, within which, by the use of submarines, she sinks, without notice. American ships and destroys American lives. . . . The first war zone was declared by Great Britain. She gave us and the world notice of it on the 4th day of November, 1914. The zone became effective Nov. 5, 1914. . . . This zone so declared by Great Britain covered the whole of the North Sea. . . . The first German war zone was declared on the 4th day of February, 1915, just three months after the British war zone was declared. Germany gave fifteen days' notice of the establishment of her zone, which became effective on the 18th day of February, 1915. The German war zone covered the English Channel and the high seawaters around the British Isles. . . .

It is unnecessary to cite authority to show that both of these orders declaring military zones were illegal and contrary to international law. It is sufficient to say that our government has officially declared both of them to be illegal and has officially protested against both of them. The only difference is that in the case of Germany we have persisted in our protest, while in the case of England we have submitted.

The United States Had Alternatives to Declaring War

What was our duty as a government and what were our rights when we were confronted with these extraordinary orders declaring these military zones? First, we could have defied both of them and could have gone to war against both of these nations for this violation of international law and interference with our neutral rights. Second, we had the technical right to defy one and to acquiesce in the other. Third, we could, while denouncing them both as illegal, have acquiesced in them both and thus remained neutral with both sides, although not agreeing with either as to the righteousness of their respective orders. We could have said to American shipowners that, while these orders are both contrary to international law and are both unjust, we do not believe that the provocation is sufficient to cause us to go to war for the defense of our rights as a neutral nation, and, therefore, American ships and American citizens will go into these zones at their own peril and risk.

An American Embargo Was One Option

Fourth, we might have declared an embargo against the shipping from American ports of any merchandise to either one of these governments that persisted in maintaining its military zone. We might have refused to permit the sailing of any ship from any American port to either of these military zones. In my judgment, if we had pursued this course, the zones would have been of short duration. England would have been compelled to take her mines out of the North Sea in order to get any supplies from our country. When her mines were taken out of the North Sea then the German ports upon the North Sea would have been accessible to American shipping and Germany would have been compelled to cease her submarine warfare in order to get any supplies from our nation into German North Sea ports.

There are a great many American citizens who feel that we owe it as a duty to humanity to take part in this war. Many instances of cruelty and inhumanity can be found on both sides. Men are often biased in their judgment on account of their sympathy and their interests. To my mind, what we ought to have maintained from the beginning was the strictest neutrality. If we had done this, I do not believe we would have been on the verge of war at the present time. We had a right as a nation, if we desired, to cease at any time to be neutral. We had a technical right to respect the English war zone and to disregard the German war zone, but we could not do that and be neutral.

The Push for War

I have no quarrel to find with the man who does not desire our country to remain neutral. While many such people are moved by selfish motives and hopes of gain, I have no doubt but that in a great many instances, through what I believe to be a misunderstanding of the real condition, there are many honest, patriotic citizens who think we ought to engage in this war and who are behind the President in his demand that we should declare war against Germany. I think such people err in judgment and to a great extent have been misled as to the real history and the true facts by the almost unanimous demand of the great combination of wealth that has a direct financial interest in our participation in the war.

To my mind, what we ought to have maintained from the beginning was the strictest neutrality. If we had done this, I do not believe we would have been on the verge of war at the present time.

We have loaned many hundreds of millions of dollars to the Allies in this controversy. While such action was legal and countenanced by international law, there is no doubt in my mind but the enormous amount of money loaned to the Allies in this country has been instrumental in bringing about a public sentiment in favor of our country taking a course that would make every bond worth a hundred cents on the dollar and making the payment of every debt certain and sure. Through this instrumentality and also through the instrumentality of others who have not only made millions out of the war in the manufacture of munitions, etc., and who would expect to make millions more if our country can be drawn into the catastrophe, a large number of the great newspapers and news agencies of the country have been controlled and enlisted in the greatest propaganda that the world has ever known to manufacture sentiment in favor of war.

We are going into war upon the command of gold.

It is now demanded that the American citizens shall be used as insurance policies to guarantee the safe delivery of munitions of war to belligerent nations. The enormous profits of munition manufacturers, stockbrokers, and bond dealers must be still further increased by our entrance into the war. This has brought us to the present moment, when Congress, urged by the President and backed by the artificial sentiment, is about to declare war and engulf our country in the greatest holocaust that the world has ever known. . . .

War Is Disastrous for the Common People

To whom does war bring prosperity? Not to the soldier who for the munificent compensation of $16 per month shoulders his musket and goes into the trench, there to shed his blood and to die if necessary; not to the brokenhearted widow who waits for the return of the mangled body of her husband; not to the mother who weeps at the death of her brave boy; not to the little children who shiver with cold; not to the babe who suffers from hunger; nor to the millions of mothers and daughters who carry broken hearts to their graves. War brings no prosperity to the great mass of common and patriotic citizens. It increases the cost of living of those who toil and those who already must strain every effort to keep soul and body together. War brings prosperity to the stock gambler on Wall Street—to those who are already in possession of more wealth than can be realized or enjoyed. . . .

Their object in having war and in preparing for war is to make money. Human suffering and the sacrifice of human life are necessary, but Wall Street considers only the dollars and the cents. The men who do the fighting, the people who make the sacrifices are the ones who will not be counted in the measure of this great prosperity that he depicts. The stockbrokers would not, of course, go to war because the very object they have in bringing on the war is profit, and therefore they must remain in their Wall Street offices in order to share in that great prosperity which they say war will bring. The volunteer officer, even the drafting officer, will not find them. They will be concealed in their palatial offices on Wall Street, sitting behind mahogany desks, covered up with clipped coupons [interest-bearing bonds]—coupons soiled with the sweat of honest toil; coupons stained with mothers' tears, coupons dyed in the lifeblood of their fellowmen.

The War Decision Is Dictated by Wall Street, Not the Masses

We are taking a step today that is fraught with untold danger. We are going into war upon the command of gold. We are going to run the risk of sacrificing millions of our countrymen's lives in order that other countrymen may coin their lifeblood into money. And even if we do not cross the Atlantic and go into the trenches, we are going to pile up a debt that the toiling masses that shall come many generations after us will have to pay. Unborn millions will bend their backs in toil in order to pay for the terrible step we are now about to take.

We are about to do the bidding of wealth's terrible mandate. By our act we will make millions of our countrymen suffer, and the consequences of it may well be that millions of our brethren must shed their lifeblood, millions of brokenhearted women must weep, millions of children must suffer with cold, and millions of babes must die from hunger, and all because we want to preserve the commercial right of American citizens to deliver munitions of war to belligerent nations.

Chapter 4

The U.S. Decision to Enter World War I in Retrospect

1

American Intervention Was Avoidable: Wilson's Neglected Options

Morton Borden and Otis L. Graham Jr.

In this excerpt from their book *Speculations on American History*, University of California at Santa Barbara historians Morton Borden and Otis L. Graham Jr. argue that President Woodrow Wilson had alternatives to the U.S. intervention against Germany in April 1917. Borden and Graham note that because presidents have extraordinary power in the field of foreign policy under the American system, Wilson had the option to choose a different path than military intervention. They note two specific actions the president might have approved that would have helped avoid American intervention in the war: a ban on munitions exports and a ban on American passenger travel on belligerent (mostly British) vessels. Wilson rejected these proposals, which had support in Congress before 1917. The authors conclude by suggesting that had the United States remained neutral, the nation could have avoided thousands of casualties, the weakening of idealism and domestic reform movements, and the repression of dissent during and after the war.

A noninterventionist course for America [in the world war] was neither impossible nor even very difficult. The circumstances of the time permitted American policymakers to make a different set of choices.

Morton Borden and Otis L. Graham Jr., *Speculations on American History*. Lexington, MA: D.C. Heath and Company, 1977. Copyright © 1977 by D.C. Heath and Company. All rights reserved. Reproduced by permission of Houghton Mifflin Company.

We may recall the major decisions that Wilson made on the road to intervention—a long one, with many twists—and the circumstances that shaped his performance as chief executive of a neutral country. When the war broke out, there appeared to be no decisions for him to make. The war was far away and, to Americans, it was pointless—a barbaric irrelevancy. Let the Europeans settle it, as they were expected to do one way or another in about six months. These were virtually every American's first reactions when the war commenced. Certainly they were Wilson's views.

British Blockade Stirs Less American Concern than German U-Boats

Yet he soon had choices to make, as we were a maritime power engaged in trans-Atlantic trade. The British began to impose an ever-tightening blockade of the Axis powers [Central Powers] to intercept goods intended for Germany which Her Majesty's government classified as "contraband" by an unprecedentedly broad definition. In this and other ways, the British began a series of violations of American neutral rights to which the Wilson administration was forced to respond. To foreshorten a long and complex story, the Americans officially complained but never pressed so hard as to endanger relations with England. At the same time, credits and then loans by private banking firms were permitted by the government, so that Anglo-American trade steadily forged an ever more substantial ligament of sympathy and common interest.

Perhaps there was no sharply different policy that could have been adopted where Britain was concerned, although some of Wilson's contemporaries thought there was. British violations of our rights were irritating but they cost no lives. The public was less than outraged. Hurt feelings were buffered by Anglophiles in the President's circle of advisers and by timely British concessions to American pride. Impoundment of ships and cargoes was never pressed to the point of justifying a breach of diplomatic relations. Dealing with Britain was not where Wilson had to make his major choices.

These hard decisions came where Germany was concerned. Blockaded and threatened with economic strangulation, the Germans built an undersea navy and turned it loose, in February 1915, upon all shipping bound for England and France. American rights were immediately challenged in the most shocking way, her citizens being killed in a series of submarine attacks upon Allied and even neutral vessels. An American was killed when the *Falaba* was sunk on March 28, more American lives were lost in the sinking of the *Cushing* and the *Gulflight* some weeks later, and on May 7 the huge Cunard liner *Lusitania* went down from one German torpedo, taking 1,198 lives, 128 of them American.

The President's Policy Options

Wilson struggled to find a way out of an admittedly untenable position. He could not simply do nothing. Press reports of American deaths at sea would eventually bring humiliation upon the head of a nation that endured such affronts without response. Ex-President Theodore Roosevelt was already raising loud criticism. There were two broad paths for Wilson to follow. A neutral nation could hope to arrange an alteration of the rules of war on the seas, so that its citizens and trade were treated with reasonable consideration; or it could unilaterally decide to keep its citizens out of harm's way by giving up travel in whatever areas the mighty antagonists of Europe chose to define as war zones.

Woodrow Wilson chose to explore the former path, and one emphasizes the word *chose*, as there were in the years 1914–17 no forces in the American political or constitutional landscape strong enough to force him one way or the other. The making of foreign policy was a presidential responsibility under the Constitution, as Wilson himself had written in *Constitutional Government in the United States* (1908) in his role as a leading constitutional scholar:

> One of the greatest of the presidential powers . . . [was] his control, which is very nearly absolute, of the foreign relations of the nation. The initiative in foreign affairs, which the President possesses without any restriction whatever, is virtually the power to control them absolutely.

This has an imperious sound, but was not far from the truth. Not once in the years 1914–17 did Congress effectively challenge either the President's right to control foreign policy or any specific policy he selected.

Obviously no President had an entirely free hand. He could not, at any time between 1914 and 1916, have secured a declaration of war, for example—on either belligerent bloc. Another foreign policy he could not undertake (in 1919–20) was official adherence to the League of Nations, although bad tactics and ill health spoiled reasonably good chances here. But between the two paths of policy previously outlined—either the search for altered and tolerable forms of oceanic warfare or the decision to forego travel in the war zone—Wilson was free to choose. There would have been some grumbling either way, but Congress—which was under Democratic majorities—would not have overruled him. As for "public opinion," it was poorly formed on international issues, and tended to be quite deferential [yielding] to the executive on international issues. In the American system, the boundaries within which foreign policies may be formulated are exceptionally wide, especially when the President is articulate and politically astute. The public is relatively well organized to influence domestic policy, but knows less about international affairs, is less confident of its judgments, and is poorly organized to participate in debate. Presidents are expected to lead. This was true in 1914–17 as it has been before and since.

Yet how was Wilson to arrange a more humane practice of naval warfare between belligerents who fought, or so they assumed, for their very survival? He began at once, acting with imagination and tenacity. In the spring of 1915, at Secretary of State William Jennings Bryan's suggestion, he proposed a *modus vivendi* [Latin: temporary agreement; compromise], by which Britain would allow noncontraband into Germany and cease her misuse of neutral flags and the arming of merchantmen, while Germany was to observe cruiser rules in submarine warfare. Cruiser rules meant adequate warning before attack so that civilians could take to life boats, or a ship could surrender. Germany appeared to agree to the *modus vivendi* but Britain found the proposal unacceptable and the idea dropped from discussion.

Wilson's Tough Talk on Submarines Backfires

Then came the *Lusitania* sinking, and Wilson decided that basic neutral rights were at stake. He began a series of stern notes to Germany which, by summer's end, had forced the Axis to lift their unrestricted submarine campaign and observe the rules of cruiser warfare, which spelled futility and often death for submarine crews.

Wilson had thus forced a major change in the conduct of naval warfare. But he quickly realized how high the cost had been. Should the Germans change their minds at any time and resume the earlier tactics, the United States would have little choice but to break off relations, arm her ships, and accept the risky role of armed neutrality. The President tried throughout 1916 to escape from the corner in which he had become trapped by the combination of global events and his own decisions. He tried to persuade the British to take all but token armaments off merchant ships, and was rebuffed. He dispatched his aide, Colonel House, to Europe in order to explore opportunities for a mediated peace. To cut short a tangled story, neither side was interested in an armistice and negotiations until it had achieved the upper hand and could dictate terms. In December 1916, Wilson issued a public appeal to the belligerents, asking them to state their terms for peace. In January, he offered himself as an impartial mediator in a speech which called for "a peace without victory." It was too late. Germany had decided upon the resumption of unrestricted submarine warfare on January 9, the new tactics to commence on February 1. For two more months, Wilson resisted a declaration of war. But there were sinkings, tensions rose, and on April 2 he asked Congress to join the conflict on the Allied side. There was a brief but heated debate, then an overwhelming vote to enter the First World War.

What Wilson Might Have Done to Avoid Intervention

Had there been any other reasonable alternatives open to Wilson along the way? There were several, and they all lay along that other path that Wilson had rejected—modifying American use of the seas rather than modifying the conduct of the belligerents' naval war. Two measures that were politically possible would probably have been enough to preserve neutrality throughout the long conflict: the elimination of munitions from trade with Europe, and a passenger ban.

The ban on munitions was proposed by Senator Gilbert Hitchcock of Nebraska as early as December 1914. It was a policy adopted by Denmark, Sweden, Italy, the Netherlands, Spain, and Norway, all without any apparent national humiliation. The ban would have altered Germany's perception of the impact of American trade, perhaps also her impression of the tenor of our neutrality. It would have somewhat eased the pressure for unrestricted submarine warfare, and aided Wilson's effort to emerge as an acceptable mediator. By itself, the munitions ban would only have ameliorated [lessened], without eliminating, the basic source of conflict between the United States and Germany, which was a trade running predominantly to the Atlantic Allies. Removing munitions from that trade was not only possible, but useful in the search for a truly neutral position. To end the trade entirely [foodstuffs, minerals, etc., as well as munitions] would have been more useful in that direction, but one can hardly call it a plausible policy. Thomas Jefferson had tried an embargo on trade a century before, in another great European war, and the economic dislocation of that policy had set up political pressures that no President could long endure.

A passenger ban would have eliminated that loss of American life which so inflamed German-American relations.

In addition to a munitions embargo, there might easily have been established a passenger ban on travel in the war zone. After the [British passenger liner] *Persia* was sunk in January 1916 [with two Americans among the 334 drowned], the principal congressional reaction was anger—but not at the Germans. The irritation was directed at an American policy that encouraged citizens to travel where they endangered both their own lives and the nation's noninvolvement. The Gore-McLemore Bill to prohibit passenger travel into the war zone had instant and overwhelming support in both Houses. Only by a supreme effort did Wilson beat it back. His reasons were both moralistic and constitutional. Rigidly and with some passion, he insisted that to withdraw unilaterally from American citizens one right that they had formerly enjoyed would cause the whole fabric of international law to crumble.

This startling idea may be understood only if one was raised, as was Wilson, in a Presbyterian [church] parsonage. Other neutral nations had banned passenger travel in the war zone without the collapse of international morality. To this unusual objection to the Gore-McLemore Bill, Wilson added the consideration that the making of foreign policy was a presidential rather than a congressional responsibility. If he allowed the bill to pass, it might be seen as a signal that Congress was now empowered to take occasional initiatives in foreign policy. Something may be said for this view, but not very much. Most contemporaries thought Wilson's views extreme, and felt that he could easily have accepted the passenger ban without damage to national honor, international law, or the Constitution. A passenger ban would have eliminated that loss of American life which so inflamed German-American relations. With this and the munitions embargo, neutrality in the long ordeal of war would rest upon much firmer foundations.

Roads Not Taken

. . . [O]ur speculations . . . suggest that history might have been very different with a change in a few decisions by essentially one person [President Woodrow Wilson]. Moments of this sort do not occur too frequently in history. When they do, decisions about war are often involved. One thinks easily of other such occasions—John Adams holding out against war in 1798–99, and Kaiser Wilhelm of Germany deciding the other way in 1914.

What if America had not joined the Great War? The costs that were paid would not have been paid, nor the benefits accrued. Another set of gains and losses would have replaced them. Perhaps it is merely the present-mindedness of a war-weary (and Cold-War weary) generation that inclines us, members of that generation, at least, to prefer the road not taken. It leads toward events that may be reconstructed only in the imagination, with fragments of facts from the past. One imagines an extended era of internal social reform, the absence of death, and the avoidance of that waste of resources, that enfeeblement of moral idealism, and that repression of dissenters in wartime America. And all that is lost on the other side of the ledger of war are those fleeting moments of moral exhilaration at Wilson's splendid cause, some experience at closer cooperation, and some crude lessons [learned from the war] in managing the economy. The situation was open for an alternative future, not vastly different from the one we lived, but different enough to stir the imagination.

2

American Intervention Was Inevitable After the Zimmermann Note Incident

Barbara W. Tuchman

Pulitzer Prize–winning historian Barbara W. Tuchman (1912–1989) believed that only through careful documentary research could a historian lay claim to a truthful account of past events. In her book *The Zimmermann Telegram* Tuchman explains how British intelligence agents intercepted, decoded, and passed on to U.S. officials a brazen telegram from German foreign secretary Arthur Zimmermann to the German ambassador in Mexico. The telegram proposed a German alliance with the Mexican government. In return for Mexico's support of Germany in its war against France and England, Germany would support Mexico against the U.S. government and help Mexico recapture California, Arizona, and New Mexico. In the excerpt that follows, Tuchman lays out the dramatic impact these revelations had on American opinion when they were made public in March 1917. Because Americans in the western states became alarmed by a potential alliance of Germany, Mexico, and Japan, they joined already anti-German East Coast Americans in calling for war. Tuchman argues that after the Zimmermann telegram episode, a reluctant President Woodrow Wilson could no longer resist the pressure for a declaration of war against Germany. Although German submarine attacks and the first Russian Revolution of March 1917 also pushed Wilson toward a decision for war, Tuchman believes that the Zimmermann telegram incident was the event that probably made full U.S. military intervention in the war inevitable.

[G]erman foreign secretary Arthur] Zimmermann's admission [on March 3, 1917, that Germany had in fact sent the intercepted cable] shattered the indifference with which three-quarters of the United States had regarded the war until that moment. The nation sat up and gasped, "They mean us!" Nothing since the outbreak of war had so openly conveyed a deliberately hostile intent toward Americans, and nothing had so startled opinion across the country. Back in 1915 the *Lusitania* had shocked the nation, but that shock was humanitarian, not personal. This was different. This was Germany proposing to attack the United States, conspiring with America's neighbor [Mexico] to snatch American territory; worse, conspiring to set an Oriental foe [Japan] upon America's back. This was a direct threat upon the body of America, which most Americans had never dreamed was a German intention. It penetrated to the midpoint of the continent, even to Omaha, Nebraska, a thousand miles from either ocean and a thousand miles from Mexico. "The issue shifts" soberly stated the Omaha *World Herald*, "from Germany against Great Britain to Germany against the United States."

The Zimmermann Intercept Hardens American Support of War

Wilson had said the American people would not believe that Germany was hostile to them "unless and until we are obliged to believe it." And, in judging the submarine issue to be no cause for believing it, the American people, on the whole, agreed with him. Torpedoings of merchant ships and loss of noncombatant lives, including American, convinced Americans of German frightfulness but not of German hostility to themselves. Despite Washington's concentration on neutral rights and freedom of the seas, the mass of Americans, who never saw a seacoast, could not be worked into war fever over an international lawyers' doctrine nor aroused to a fighting mood over persons who chose to cross the ocean on belligerent boats in wartime. Besides, they had got used to maritime atrocities, had grown accustomed to official crises over ship sinkings. The *Lusitania*, the *Sussex*, the *Arabic* had followed one after another, provoking Wilson's notes, [Secretary of State William Jennings] Bryan's resignation, endless correspondence in incomprehensible diplomatic language, even some quite comprehensible threats and ultimatums, all mixed up with similar eruptions vis-à-vis the British over contraband and blacklisting [British boycotting of U.S. companies that traded with Germany]. It was all very confusing and—to the majority of the country—remote.

If Wilson does not go to war now, [Theodore Roosevelt] wrote to [Senator Henry Cabot] Lodge, "I shall skin him alive."

But the Prussian [German] Invasion Plot, as the newspapers labeled the Zimmermann telegram, was clear as a knife in the back and near as next door. Everybody understood it in an instant. When Germany plotted attack upon United States territory there could no longer be any question of neutrality. Overnight the Midwest isolationist press acknowledged it. The Chicago *Daily Tribune* warned its readers they must realize now, "without delay, that Germany recognizes us as an enemy," and the United States could no longer expect to keep out of "active participation in the present conflict." The Cleveland *Plain Dealer* said there was "neither virtue nor dignity" in refusing to fight now. The Oshkosh [Wisconsin] *Northwestern* said the note had turned pacifists, critics, and carpers into patriots overnight. The Detroit *Times* said, "It looks like war for this country." All these papers had been ardently neutral until Zimmermann shot an arrow in the air and brought down neutrality like a dead duck.

His admission exploded the disbelief in the telegram which the pacifists and pro-Germans had clung to when the blow first fell upon them. [German-American spokesman] George Sylvester Viereck said it ended pro-Germanism in the United States. Nothing the American government could have said could have convinced the doubters, but when Zimmermann said, "It is true," he himself silenced the talk of forgery and British trick. The German-Americans, of whom he had such fond hopes, retreated across their hyphen to take their stand, somewhat sullenly, on the American side. In Minneapolis, where large numbers of them were concentrated, the *Journal* admitted it was no longer possible for German-Americans to be loyal to both their native and their adopted countries, and the *Tribune* said Germany's bid to bring in Japan against us was "equivalent to an act of war." In Milwaukee, home of the German brewing industry, that city's *Journal* feared that Zimmermann's act would cause a "revulsion of sentiment" among Germany's many friends in the Middle West, and this proved to be the case. Such papers as the Chicago *Staats-Zeitung*, the Detroit *Abend-Post*, the Cincinnati *Volksblatt* and *Freie Presse*, and the St. Louis *Amerika*, several of which had earlier pronounced the telegram a fraud, were now sheepishly silent or hurried to proclaim their loyalty to America.

The telegram was not the only deciding factor upon the President. It was, rather, the last drop that emptied his cup of neutrality.

Midwest sentiment paled beside the outraged indignation of the Pacific Coast and the roar that came out of Texas. The San Antonio *Light* asserted with "quiet modesty and simple truth" that if a German-Mexican-Japanese army overran Texas, not a Texan would be left alive unless he was across the border fighting his way back. The El Paso *Times* grew purple at the spectacle of Prussian [German] militarism "writhing in the slime of intrigue," and out in California the Sacramento *Bee* echoed its outrage at Germany's "treacherous enmity, underhanded, nasty intriguing."

Editors from Vermont to Florida to Oregon expressed a sense of Zimmermann's having crystallized feelings everywhere. The Springfield (Massachusetts) *Republican* said that nothing else but this threat of hostile action to American territory could have so solidified the American people, and the Los Angeles *Tribune* said it extinguished all differences. These were overstatements, because editorial opinion never truly reflects the diversity of private opinions. Pacifism was not extinguished, but it was outweighed by a sense that America was now involved and, willing or not, would have to fight.

In the already Anglophile East the press tended to regard the Zimmermann note as a blessing that would awaken the rest of the country to an awareness of the German threat, and the Eastern papers did their best to warm up that awareness. The Buffalo *Express* let itself go in a horrendous imagining of "hordes of Mexicans under German officers, sweeping into Texas, New Mexico and Arizona." The New York *American* on its own authority added Russia to the proposed combination of Germany, Mexico, and Japan, and depicted this unholy quadruple alliance overwhelming and carving up our country: Mexico, it said, would retake the Southwest and restore it to barbarism; Japan would take the Far West and "orientalize" it; Germany and Russia would enslave generations of Americans in the payment of vast war indemnities. "Citizens, prepare!" it commanded. "The hours are short, the days are few. . . ."

By the middle of March, when the Zimmermann telegram had had two weeks to take effect, the American people, by and large, realized they would have to face up to war. The press was already ahead of the President. Individual pacifists were still vocal, but the majority of the people were mentally (if not militarily) prepared. They were not calling for war; they were simply waiting—waiting for Wilson. Far in the van, Theodore Roosevelt was bugling for action. If Germany's plot to get Mexico and Japan to join her in "dismembering" this country was not an overt act of war, he told a public meeting, then Lexington and Bunker Hill (rather an odd comparison) were not overt acts of war. If Wilson does not go to war now, he wrote to [Senator Henry Cabot] Lodge, "I shall skin him alive.". . .

The American Path Toward War

While Zimmermann was still trying to draw in Mexico, events in America were hurrying toward the brink. On March 4 [1917] Congress, gagged by . . . [a] Senate filibuster, had gone out of session without passing the Armed Ship Bill [a Wilson administration proposal to arm American merchant ships for defense against German submarines]. Wilson raged at the American government's being thus rendered "helpless and contemptible" by "a little band of willful men representing no opinion but their own." An extra session, required by the Senate's refusal to vote the appropriation bills, was scheduled to convene on April 16 so that the country would not be left, as Lodge said, "alone with Wilson" for nine months. Until it met again, the President held the helm alone. On March 9, using his executive authority, he gave the order to arm the ships anyway. He did not, however, take any action on an urgent message from [U.S. ambassador to Britain Walter H.] Page warning that, failing a United States government loan, Britain could not buy another gun or crate of goods from America.

On March 18 three American ships were sunk without warning by U-boats. On March 19 occurred the most significant event of the war prior to America's entrance—the preliminary revolution in Russia that overthrew the [autocratic] Czar and established the parliamentary Kerensky government. With the disappearance of the Czar, the black sheep vanished from the democratic herd and the war could now be safely said to be a war to save democracy. On March 20 the President met the Cabinet and heard them unanimously declare for war, even including the pacifist [Secretary of the Navy Josephus] Daniels, who was close to tears. As was his habit, Wilson left the room without declaring himself. That night he must have made up his mind. The next day, March 21, he reconvened Congress for April 2, two weeks earlier than scheduled, to hear a message concerning "grave matters of national policy."

In itself the Zimmermann telegram was only a pebble on the long road of history. But a pebble can kill a Goliath, and this one killed the American illusion that we could go about our business happily separate from other nations.

The night before he spoke the public words that were to mark a chasm in our history, he spoke other words to a friend, Frank Cobb, the liberal editor of the New York *World*, whom he asked to visit him at the White House. They have the quality of last words, like Sir Walter Raleigh's poem before his execution. He could see no alternative, Wilson said, although he had tried every way he knew to avoid war. He said that once the American people entered the war, freedom and tolerance and level-headedness would be forgotten. Moreover, a declaration of war would mean "that Germany would be beaten and so badly beaten that there would be a dictated peace, a victorious peace. . . . At the end of the war there will be no bystanders with sufficient power to influence the terms. There won't be any peace standards left to work with." And even at this moment the cry broke from him, "If there is any alternative, for God's sake, let's take it!"

Wilson's Electrifying War Message

But there was none. At eight-thirty next evening he drove up to the Capitol through the rain and went in to face a joint session. "With a profound sense of the solemn and even tragical character of the step I am taking," he advised Congress to "declare the recent course of the Imperial German Government to be in fact nothing less than war against the government and people of the United States," and to "formally accept the status of belligerent." Neutrality, he said, is no longer possible or desirable under the menace that lies "in the existence of autocratic governments backed by organized force which is controlled wholly by their will and not by the will of the people." He dwelt on the submarines as outlaws against the law of nations and on other proofs of the German government's intention to act against the security of the United States, referring specifically to the Zimmermann telegram. "That it [the German government] means to stir up enemies against us at our very doors, the intercepted note to the German Minister at Mexico is eloquent evidence. We accept this challenge of hostile purpose. . . ."

Packed into the chamber, the members of both Houses, the Supreme Court, the Cabinet, the diplomatic corps, the press, and the visitors who filled the gallery listened with every nerve. The peroration [conclusion of the speech] mounted to the phrases that everyone knows, as the speaker declared that the German government was a "natural foe of liberty," that "the world must be made safe for democracy," that "the right is more precious than peace," that America must fight "for the principles that gave her birth," that, "God helping her, she can do no other."

"A roar like a storm" greeted the President's address, wrote one reporter. Overseas the Allies heard it, in their moment of extremity. England, the fulcrum of the Allies, was bending; France was weakened to the point of exhaustion. Stalemated in the trenches, torpedoed on the seas, emptied of funds, they heard the sound of a huge, fresh, new ally coming to join them with ships and money and goods and men. The sound brought them the promise of victory. To an English historian, R.B. Mowat, the event was "one of the most dramatic in history."

Why a Reluctant Wilson Chose War

To Americans it was the beginning of unwilled wedlock to the rest of the world. The question, what brought it about? has been asked ever since. Why did Wilson, who three months earlier had said it would be a "crime against civilization" to lead the United States into war, who cried out for an alternative even on the eve of war, decide at last that "the right is more precious than peace"? His April 2 summary of the nature of the enemy as "the natural foe of liberty" was equally true three months or six months, a year or two years earlier. The man who made the April 2 speech was the same man who wished to settle for peace without victory in January, who refused to believe that the Germans were hostile to us in February. Ambassador Page, writing in his diary, asks the inevitable question, "What made him change his mind? Just when and how did the President come to see the true nature of the Germans?" Was it Germany's declaration of unrestricted U-boat war on February 1 or was it, Page wondered, the Zimmermann telegram?

Certainly it was not the former, for the President had refused to believe that the Germans meant to do what they declared they would until they should prove it by an "overt act." This came on March 18, when the three American merchant ships were sunk with heavy loss of life. Within the next three days followed the solemn Cabinet meeting and the President's summons to Congress, which marks the point when he made up his mind. Would he have decided as he did without the telegram with its earlier revelation of Germany's overt hostility to America? Only Wilson can answer that, and he never did. One answer has been offered by a man whom the President trusted and made the recipient of all his [presidential] papers. When Wilson, in the last letter he ever wrote, a week before his death [in 1924], asked Ray Stannard Baker to write his official biography, he said, "I would rather have your interpretation than that of anyone else I know." Baker's judgment of the Zimmermann telegram is that "no single more devastating blow was delivered against Wilson's resistance to entering the war."

This is not to say that Wilson wanted neutrality the day before the telegram, and belligerency the day after. The telegram was not the only deciding factor upon the President. It was, rather, the last drop that emptied his cup of neutrality.

There were other factors too, not the least "the wonderful and heartening" overturn in Russia [the Russian Revolution], which, he told Congress, now made that great nation "a fit partner for a League of Honor." Probably the nearest one can approximate the truth about what moved Wilson is to say that a combination of events brought him to a point where he had no alternative. As Lodge said, he was in the grip of events. As England's outspoken Lord Chancellor, Lord Birkenhead, said, "The United States were in fact kicked into the war against the strong and almost frenzied efforts of President Wilson."

Zimmermann Telegram: The Immediate Cause of U.S. Intervention

The kick that did it, to the people whether or not to the President, was the Zimmermann telegram. It awoke that part of the country that had been undecided or indifferent before. It transformed, Lansing said, the apathy of the Western states into "intense hostility to Germany" and "in one day accomplished a change in sentiment and public opinion that otherwise would have required months to accomplish." It was not a theory or an issue but an unmistakable gesture that anyone could understand. It was the German boot planted upon our [southwest] border. To the mass of Americans, who cared little and thought less about Europe, it meant that if they fought they would be fighting to defend America, not merely to extract Europe from its self-made quarrels. It put them in a frame of mind willing to accept Wilson's statement in April of the necessity of war.

Would they have been ready without the telegram? Probably not. Before it was published, the dominant feeling inspired by the war—always excepting pro-Ally New England—was the stubborn, if inglorious, slogan that elected Wilson four months before—"He kept us out of war." Afterward, so far as public organs of opinion can reveal it, the mood changed to one of recognition that war could no longer be evaded. Wilson knew this when he drafted his speech for the meeting of Congress on April 2. He knew that what he had to say would be accepted; that, in fact, he no longer had any excuse for not saying it. Until then he could afford to ignore all the goading of the Lodge and Roosevelt forces because he knew the country as a whole was not with them. After the public reaction to the Zimmermann telegram, even that excuse was taken from him. On March 17 the *Literary Digest* published a résumé of nationwide press comment on the telegram under the heading, "How Zimmermann United the United States." That was a fair estimate of published opinion, even if it ignored the unswerving [antiwar] LaFollettes and Norrises and Villards and that mute opinion which can never be weighed. It left Wilson bereft [deprived] of the prop of public opinion which had so far sustained his struggle to keep the United States neutral. After the middle of March there was nothing to hold him back.

Had the telegram never been intercepted or never been published, inevitably the Germans would have done something else that would have brought us in eventually. But the time was already late and, had we delayed much longer, the Allies might have been forced to negotiate. To that extent the Zimmermann telegram altered the course of history. But then, as Sir Winston Churchill has remarked, the course of history is always being altered by something or other—if not by a horseshoe nail, then by an intercepted telegram. In itself the Zimmermann telegram was only a pebble on the long road of history. But a pebble can kill a Goliath, and this one killed the American illusion that we could go about our business happily separate from other nations. In world affairs it was a German Minister's minor plot. In the lives of the American people it was the end of innocence.

3

Historians Debate the U.S. Entry into World War I

Robert D. Schulzinger

In 1917 President Woodrow Wilson led the United States into war against Germany. Historians have debated the reasons for his decision ever since. In the following selection, historian Robert D. Schulzinger traces the history of this debate, showing how the arguments have changed over the decades since the war. Initially, most historians accepted Wilson's argument that the United States had to enter the war to protect democracy for itself and the rest of the world. By the 1920s and 1930s, however, more skeptical "revisionist" historians turned to economic explanations of America's intervention. During the Great Depression many Americans blamed the 1917 intervention on the "merchants of death"—pro-Allies U.S. munition makers and bankers who profited from the war. During World War II, the revisionist viewpoint fell into disfavor as the war strengthened people's beliefs that the United States must play a central role in reforming the world order. By the 1960s and 1970s, both defenders and critics of the decision to enter World War I could agree that Wilson was a formidable figure whose ideas and policies merited respect, but they sharply diverged in their opinions about his legacy. Schulzinger's fundamental argument is that perspectives on any key event like World War I change with the times. Robert D. Schulzinger teaches history at the University of Colorado and has written extensively on twentieth-century American diplomatic history. He is the author of *A Time for War: The United States and Viet-*

Robert D. Schulzinger, *U.S. Diplomacy Since 1900*. New York: Oxford University Press, 2002. Copyright © 1984 by Oxford University Press, Inc. Reproduced by permission.

nam, 1941–1975 and *The Wise Men of Foreign Affairs: The History of the Council on Foreign Relations.*

Entry into World War I marked a great departure in United States foreign relations. Americans knew that at the time and have argued over it ever since, asking why Wilson made his decision, questioning his reasoning, and proposing alternatives. These arguments represent more than making work for professors filling learned journals with complicated theories; the memory of how the United States fought in 1917 affected the conduct of American diplomacy for generations.

Postwar "Revisionist" Writers Raise Doubts About 1917

Woodrow Wilson's official biographer, journalist Ray Stannard Baker, presented a standard interpretation in the 1920s when he argued in *Woodrow Wilson* that the president abandoned neutrality for belligerency for exactly the reasons he cited in his [April 1917 war] message. Unrestricted submarine warfare represented a "barbarous" affront to international law, and the United States fought to preserve its traditional understanding of the rights of neutrals. Stress on [such] eighteenth-century rights seemed outmoded even as Baker wrote, for many American liberals had become disillusioned with the failures of Wilson's diplomacy to achieve any real improvements in world politics in the twenties. During the twenties, liberals licked wounds and punctured pompous pretensions; a decade later, during the Depression, their views received a sympathetic hearing. Stressing economic factors and the malevolent influence of bankers and munitions manufacturers, a school of "revisionists" carried the day after 1919. Such writers as Harry Elmer Barnes (*Genesis of the World War* [1926]), Charles Tansill (*America Goes to War* [1938]), C. Hartley Grattan (*Why We Fought* [1929]), and J. Kenneth Tunnef (*Shall It Be Again?* [1922]) shifted the focus from President Wilson, whom they considered sanctimonious and slow, to the house of Morgan [New York investment bank] and the Bethlehem Steel Company, which they charged with leading the country into combat to protect their investments in

British securities. In the midst of the Depression, two re-
porters, H.C. Engelbrecht and F.C. Hanighen, published
Merchants of Deaths an account of influence exercised by
arms manufacturers and the bankers who financed the war
efforts of the European belligerents. They argued that
Britain and France purchased cannon, ships, ammunition,
or the steel to make them in the United States with money
supplied by New York lenders. By late 1916, it appeared
that Germany might win the war, in which case loans never
would be repaid and future deliveries cancelled. To keep
business humming and assure repayment, a cabal of industrialists and bankers persuaded President Wilson's closest
advisers that the United States should join forces with the
allies against Germany. The idea that a business conspiracy
led an unwitting nation into bloodshed attracted congressional interest in 1934 when a special committee, chaired
by Progressive Republican senator Gerald Nye of North
Dakota, investigated the origins of the 1917 war. Nye's
panel assailed businessmen, whose reputation in the midst
of the Depression had reached new lows anyway, for mis-
leading the country into war, and prepared the ground for
revised neutrality laws [enacted by Congress after 1935] de-
signed to prevent a recurrence.

Word War II Invites Further Reconsideration of Wilson's Decision

By the time the United States fought the Second World
War, conventional wisdom had turned again, as Americans
once again saw Germany as a threat. In 1941, the struggles
of 1917 seemed less futile, although few students paid much
attention to legalistic quarrels over the rights of neutrals.
"Geopolitics," the study of the importance of geography
and might in world affairs, dominated the serious study of
international relations in the era of the Second World War,
and it affected the interpretations of the entry into the First.
Walter Lippmann, active as a thrice-weekly columnist for
the *New York Herald Tribune*, presented a new gloss on
American neutrality in a book he wrote in 1943, *American
Foreign Policy: Shield of the Republic*. He acknowledged that
Wilson thought he had fought for neutral rights, and he
chastised the president for excessive legalism. Lippmann
claimed that the country fought the right enemy for the
wrong reasons, and he would have preferred to have seen

the president base his message on the physical threat posed by imperial Germany.

Stressing economic factors and the malevolent influence of bankers and munitions manufacturers [on the Wilson administration], a school of "revisionists" carried the day after 1919.

Lippmann's interpretation attracted sympathetic followers among such advocates of "realism" in foreign affairs as [renowned diplomat and historian] George Kennan (*American Diplomacy*), [political scientist] Hans Morgenthau (*In Defense of the National Interest*), and [political scientist] Robert Endicott Osgood (*Ideals and Self Interest in America's Foreign Relations*) in the 1950s. None of the realists had anything good to say about Wilson, for while they thought the United States should have fought the First World War, they argued that Wilson did more harm than good by basing his decision on the rights of neutrals. Force and power were things which set the realists' blood racing.

Revisionists of the Vietnam Era

Almost inevitably, the pendulum swung back in favor of an appreciation of the subtleties of Wilson's mind. What was surprising was that both Wilson's admirers and his detractors in the sixties and seventies gave him credit for a shrewd grasp of what went on in the world. According to Arthur Link, the president's fullest biographer, his diplomacy represented a "higher realism" and an appreciation of what the world might be like if American power were applied effectively. For Link in *Wilson the Diplomatist* (1956) or *Woodrow Wilson: Revolution, War and Peace* (1979), the president's view of foreign affairs did not look backward to the classical age of neutrality but forward to a world reformed through American guidance. Patrick Devlin, a British writer who also thought well of Wilson despite misgivings about the brittleness of his character, came to essentially the same conclusions in *Too Proud to Fight* (1975).

Revisionists on the left, led by [historian] William Appleman Williams, paid Wilson the respect of taking his

ideas seriously while disapproving of the results of his policies. In *The Tragedy of American Diplomacy* (1962), Williams
rejected the earlier revisionist claim that the president was
led by the nose by the "merchants of death." Instead,
Williams insisted that Wilson made the decision on his own
to expand American influence in the emerging interdepen-
dent world economy. [Historian] N. Gordon Levin followed
a similar path in *Woodrow Wilson and World Politics* (1968),
where he suggested that Wilson set the stage for subsequent
American thought on politics. Levin felt Wilson was committed to a belief in American "exceptionalism" [a viewpoint
that the United States is the world's examplar of liberal democratic values and has a mission to extend these globally] and
certain that the United States had the power to act as the
balance wheel of international politics, and he accused Wilson of bringing the United States into war to apply his no-
tions of "liberalcapitalist-internationalism" around the
world. Williams and Levin both wrote that Wilson's expan-
sionism left a bitter legacy. From this modern revisionist
point of view, Wilsonianism encouraged Americans to embark on a fruitless quest to create stability, put down revolution, and expand American commerce. While saddened by
the results, Williams, Levin, and other revisionists respected
Wilson as a serious thinker on international affairs who led
the country into war with his eyes open to the consequences.

Whatever their differing interpretations of the reasons
for American involvement in the Great War, historians
agree that the decisions of 1916 and 1917 prepared the way
for most of what came afterward in the history of American
foreign relations. Once the United States joined the fight,
Americans no longer were special, despite what they might
think to themselves or say to others. The United States had
become a great power like the others.

Chronology

June 28, 1914
The assassination in Sarajevo of Archduke Franz Ferdinand, heir to the Hapsburg monarchy of Austria-Hungary, by a Serbian nationalist sets in motion the series of events that initiate World War I.

July 28, 1914
Austria-Hungary declares war on Serbia.

July 30, 1914
Russia moblizes its military forces.

August 1, 1914
Germany declares war on Russia.

August 3, 1914
Germany declares war on France; its troops enter neutral Belgium, prompting an ultimatum from Great Britain.

August 4, 1914
Great Britain declares war on Germany. President Woodrow Wilson formally proclaims American neutrality in the war.

August 15, 1914
The U.S. government announces that loans to belligerents violate American neutrality.

August 20, 1914
The British government issues a broad definition of war contraband and declares its intention to intercept American ships bound for Germany.

November 3, 1914
The British government declares the North Sea a war zone and begins to mine its waters.

December 29, 1914
Wilson protests British detention of American ships in search of contraband.

February 4, 1915
Germany declares a war zone around the British Isles to begin on February 18.

February 10, 1915
The State Department formally protests the German declaration of a war zone and declares that the Berlin government will be held to "strict accountability" if American ships are sunk.

March 1, 1915
A German torpedo sinks the British passenger liner *Falaba*; one American citizen is killed in the attack.

March 11, 1915
The British government announces its blockade of German ports; Wilson issues a formal protest of the blockade on March 30.

April 11, 1915
The German ambassador to the United States calls on Americans to stop exporting arms to the Allies.

April 26, 1915
France, Russia, Italy, and Great Britain conclude the secret treaty of London.

May 7, 1915
The British passenger liner *Lusitania* is sunk without warning by a German submarine, killing 1,198 people, including 128 Americans. Wilson responds by declaring in a May 10 speech that the United States is "too proud to fight."

May 13, 1915
The Wilson administration issues its first diplomatic response to the sinking of the *Lusitania*, upholding the "indisputable" right of American citizens to travel the high seas and demanding reparations from Germany.

June 6, 1915
Unwilling to provoke the United States, the German government issues a secret order to submarine commanders to spare passenger liners from torpedo attacks.

August 4, 1915
The United States receives Britain's response to blockade protests; Great Britain defends its blockade as legal but offers to submit disputed cases of seizure to arbitration.

August 19, 1915
In violation of secret instructions, a German submarine sinks the British passenger ship *Arabic*; two American citizens die.

September 1915
Wilson reverses previous policy and permits private American firms to lend money to the Allies.

September 1, 1915
Germany agrees in the *Arabic* pledge to sink no more passenger liners without warning; the pledge, made public on October 15, is viewed as a diplomatic victory for America.

December 7, 1915
Wilson addresses Congress and urges legislation that would provide for major expansion of the army and navy.

February 21, 1916
The monumental Battle of Verdun begins; it will last for ten months and claim a million French and German casualties.

March 24, 1916
In violation of the *Arabic* pledge, a German submarine torpedoes an unarmed French passenger ship, the *Sussex*, as it crosses the English Channel; several Americans are injured, none fatally.

April 18, 1916
Secretary of State Lansing warns the German government that further acts of submarine warfare will lead to the severing of diplomatic relations between the two countries.

May 4, 1916
The German government responds to Secretary Lansing by announcing that there will be no further surprise submarine attacks against either merchant ships or passenger liners. However, Germany reserves the right to use submarines in self-defense.

July 1, 1916
The Battle of the Somme begins; the British suffer more than sixty thousand casualties on the first day.

July 18, 1916
The British government issues a blacklist of some eighty American firms or individuals who may not engage in trade with Great Britain because of their German connections.

August 29, 1916
The Council of National Defense is established; it consists of six cabinet members under the direction of Secretary of War Baker and is charged with coordinating industry and resources.

August 31, 1916
Germany announces a suspension of submarine attacks.

October 15, 1916
Germany resumes submarine attacks under search-and-destroy rules.

November 7, 1916
Wilson, campaigning on a "He kept us out of war" slogan, is reelected to a second term.

December 12, 1916
The German government issues a statement indicating a willingness to discuss peace terms.

December 18, 1916
Wilson sends a note to the warring countries offering American services as a mediator and asking them to state their conditions for peace negotiations. The British angrily, but wrongly, assume that this note has been coordinated with the German statement of December 12.

January 16, 1917
German foreign minister Arthur Zimmermann sends a coded telegram to the German minister in Mexico instructing him to propose a German-Mexican alliance that could possibly lead to Mexico's recovery of territory lost to the United States during the Mexican War.

January 22, 1917
After his mediation efforts have been rebuffed, Wilson delivers his "peace without victory" speech to Congress, in

which he calls on all warring parties to settle for less than victory.

January 31, 1917
Germany resumes unrestricted submarine warfare, meaning that American and all other neutral ships traveling within war zones are subject to attack without warning.

February 3, 1917
The United States breaks off diplomatic relations with Germany.

February 26, 1917
Wilson asks Congress to pass legislation arming American merchant ships for defense against submarines.

March 1, 1917
The contents of the Zimmermann telegram (which had been intercepted by the British and passed on to the U.S. government) are revealed to the American press by the State Department.

March 12, 1917
After failing to get Senate approval, Wilson announces the arming of merchant ships by executive order.

March 29, 1917
Wilson calls for a national army to be "raised and maintained exclusively by selective draft."

March 31, 1917
The General Munitions Board is established by the Council on National Defense to coordinate war industries and military procurement; its abilities are hampered by lack of enforcement authority.

April 1, 1917
Wilson is informed that the American army is able to muster 5,791 officers and 121,797 enlisted men; during the war the number of men in the army will grow to 4 million.

April 2, 1917
Wilson asks for an American declaration of war against Germany.

April 4, 1917
The Senate votes for war, 82-6.

April 6, 1917
The House of Representatives votes for war, 373-50.

April 14, 1917
The Committee on Public Information is established by executive order; it is charged with rallying American public opinion behind the war.

April 24, 1917
Wilson signs the Liberty Loan Act; Five Liberty Loan drives will eventually net $21.4 billion. American destroyers are dispatched to the war zone.

May 18, 1917
Wilson signs the Selective Service Act, which has passed both houses of Congress by large majorities.

June 5, 1917
National draft registration day is held; more than 10 million men ages twenty-one to thirty register at over four thousand polling places across the country.

June 15, 1917
Congress passes the Espionage Act; the law specifies penalties for spies and people found guilty of aiding the enemy or obstructing conscription or military recruiting. It also empowers the postmaster general to ban from the mail periodicals and other materials deemed subversive.

June 26, 1917
First American troops arrive in France.

July 2, 1917
Pershing requests that the United States raise an army of 1 million soldiers; a few days later he increases his request to 3 million.

July 19, 1917
The German Reichstag passes a resolution calling for peace without annexations or indemnities.

July 28, 1917
The War Industries Board is established by the Council of National Defense to replace the General Munitions Board.

October 3, 1917
Congress passes the War Revenue Act, authorizing a graduated income tax that is to be the chief source of government revenue during the war.

November 7, 1917
The Bolsheviks, led by Lenin and Leon Trotsky, seize power in Russia and declare for peace.

December 7, 1917
The United States declares war on Austria-Hungary.

December 26, 1917
In its most extreme single wartime mobilization action, the federal government takes over management of the nation's railways.

January 18, 1918
Wilson delivers his "Fourteen Points" address to a joint session of Congress, describing his vision of an American peace program.

March 3, 1918
Russia (now the Soviet Union) and the Central Powers sign the Treaty of Brest-Litovsk, ending their state of war.

March 21, 1918
Reinforced by troops from the east, Germany launches a massive attack on the western front.

May 16, 1918
Congress passes the Sedition Act, which amends and strengthens the Espionage Act.

September 1918
A deadly influenza epidemic strikes the United States; three hundred thousand die within the next eight weeks.

September 26, 1918
The final Allied offensive of the war, and the one in which Americans see the most action, begins; the Meuse-Argonne offensive will continue until the war ends in November.

October 6, 1918
Germany and Austria-Hungary send notes to President Wilson requesting an armistice.

October 21, 1918
Germany unilaterally ends unrestricted submarine warfare.

November 5, 1918
Midterm elections give Republicans control of Congress.

November 9, 1918
Kaiser Wilhelm II of Germany abdicates and flees to Holland.

November 11, 1918
An armistice ending the fighting of World War I is reached after Germany asks for peace on the basis of Wilson's Fourteen Points.

December 13, 1918
Wilson arrives in France as head of the American peace delegation.

January 18, 1919
The Paris Peace Conference begins without representatives from the Central Powers.

January 25, 1919
Delegates to the conference formally approve Wilson's request that the League of Nations be made an integral part of the peace treaty.

May 7, 1919
The Treaty of Versailles is submitted to the German delegation.

June 4, 1919
Congress passes a constitutional amendment to enfranchise women, pending ratification by the states.

June 28, 1919
The Treaty of Versailles is signed by Germany and the Allies. The treaty, which features the creation of the League of Nations as its centerpiece, needs Senate ratification to take effect in the United States.

September 3, 1919
Wilson embarks on a nationwide tour to gain support for the Treaty of Versailles and for the League of Nations.

September 25, 1919

An exhausted Wilson cancels the remainder of his tour; soon after he suffers a debilitating stroke.

November 19, 1919

Henry Cabot Lodge attaches fourteen reservations to the Treaty of Versailles and submits it to the Senate for ratification. By a vote of 55-39, the Senate rejects the treaty.

March 19, 1920

The Senate holds two final votes on the Treaty of Versailles, one with and one without the Lodge reservations. Both fall short of ratification.

May 1920

Congress passes a joint resolution formally declaring an end to hostilities with Germany and Austria-Hungary; the resolution is vetoed by Wilson.

July 1920

The Democrats nominate James Cox of Ohio and Franklin Roosevelt of New York for president and vice president on a platform calling for the election to be a "solemn referendum" on the treaty and the League.

November 2, 1920

Republican Warren G. Harding is elected president; his election signals a rejection of "Wilsonian" dreams of a new international order.

July 2, 1921

Harding signs a congressional joint resolution declaring an end to war with Germany.

For Further Research

General Studies of the World War I Era

Martin Gilbert, *The First World War: A Complete History.* New York: Holt, 1994.

John Keegan, *An Illustrated History of the First World War.* New York: Knopf, 2001.

Michael J. Lyons, *World War I: A Short History.* Englewood Cliffs, NJ: Prentice-Hall, 1994.

A.J.P. Taylor, ed., *History of the First World War.* London: Octopus, 1974.

Jay Winter and Blaine Baggett, *The First World War and the Shaping of the Twentieth Century.* New York: Penguin, 1996.

The United States and World War I: 1914–1917

Lloyd Ambrosius, *Wilsonian Statecraft: The Theory and Practice of Liberal Internationalism During World War I.* Wilmington, DE: SR Books, 1991.

Thomas A. Bailey and Paul Ryan, *The Lusitania Disaster.* New York: Free Press, 1975.

John W. Chambers II, ed., *The Eagle and the Dove: The American Peace Movement and United States Foreign Policy, 1900–1922.* Syracuse, NY: Syracuse University Press, 1992.

Charles Chatfield, *For Peace and Justice: Pacifism in America, 1914–1941.* Knoxville: University of Tennessee Press, 1971.

Warren Cohen, *The American Revisionists: The Lessons of Intervention in World War I.* Chicago: University of Chicago Press, 1966.

John W. Coogan, *The End of Neutrality: The United States, Britain, and Maritime Rights, 1899–1915.* Ithaca, NY, and London: Cornell University Press, 1981.

John Milton Cooper Jr., *The Vanity of Power: American Isolationism and the First World War.* Westport, CT: Greenwood, 1969.

Patrick Devlin, *Too Proud to Fight: Woodrow Wilson's Neutrality.* Oxford, UK: Oxford University Press, 1975.

John Esposito, *The Legacy of Woodrow Wilson: American War Aims in World War I.* Westport, CT: Praeger, 1996.

John Patrick Finnegan, *Against the Specter of a Dragon: The Campaign Against Military Preparedness.* Westport, CT: Greenwood, 1974.

Otis L. Graham Jr., ed., *The Great Campaigns: Reform and War in America, 1900–1928.* Huntington, NY: Robert E. Krieger, 1980.

Ross Gregory, *The Origins of American Intervention in the First World War.* New York: W.W. Norton, 1971.

Meirion Harries and Susie Harries, *The End of Innocence: America at War, 1917–1918.* New York: Random House, 1997.

Thomas J. Knock, *To End All Wars: Woodrow Wilson and the Quest for a New World Order.* New York: Oxford University Press, 1992.

N. Gordon Levin Jr., *Woodrow Wilson and World Politics: America's Response to War and Revolution.* New York: Oxford University Press, 1968.

Arthur S. Link, *Woodrow Wilson: Revolution, War, and Peace.* Arlington Heights, IL: AHM, 1979.

———, *Woodrow Wilson and the Progressive Era, 1910–1917.* New York: Harper, 1954.

Roland Marchand, *The American Peace Movement and Social Reform, 1898–1918.* Princeton, NJ: Princeton University Press, 1972.

Henry F. May, *The End of American Innocence.* New York: Knopf, 1959.

Ernest A. McKay, *Against Wilson and War, 1914–1917.* Malabar, FL: Krieger, 1996.

Diana Preston, *Lusitania: An Epic Tragedy.* New York: Walker, 2002.

Daniel M. Smith, *The Great Departure: The United States and World War I, 1914–1920.* New York: Wiley, 1965.

Page Smith, *America Enters the World.* New York: McGraw-Hill, 1985.

Samuel R. Spencer Jr., *Decision for War, 1917.* Peterborough, NH: Bauhan, 1968.

Barbara W. Tuchman, *The Zimmermann Telegram.* New York: Macmillan, 1958.

Websites

The American Experience: Woodrow Wilson, www.pbs.org/wgbh/amex/wilson. This website is connected with a PBS video series on American presidents. It explores many facets of Wilson's life and career, including his role in World War I.

The Great War and the Shaping of the Twentieth Century, www.pbs.org/greatwar. Explores the history and effects of World War I. The emphasis is on the social, cultural, and personal impact of the war, although the military and political aspects are also thoroughly covered.

The World War I Document Archive, www.lib.byu.edu/~rdh/wwi. This site has hundreds of documents and thousands of images relating to World War I, with an emphasis on military, diplomatic, and political dimensions of the war.

Index